THE
ECONOMIC
SURPLUS

THE ECONOMIC SURPLUS

Theory, Measurement, Applications

Anders Danielson

Westport, Connecticut
London

Library of Congress Cataloging-in-Publication Data

Danielson, Anders.
    The economic surplus : theory, measurement, applications / by
  Anders Danielson.
       p. cm.
  Includes bibliographical references and index.
  ISBN 0–275–94765–3 (alk. paper)
    1. Surplus (Economics) 2. Economic development. 3. Jamaica—
  Economic conditions. I. Title.
  HB203.D36   1994
  338.9—dc20   93–37880

British Library Cataloguing in Publication Data is available.

Library of Congress Catalog Card Number: 93–37880
ISBN: 0–275–94765–3

First published in 1994

Praeger Publishers, 88 Post Road West, Westport, CT 06881
An imprint of Greenwood Publishing Group, Inc.

Printed in the United States of America

The paper used in this book complies with the
Permanent Paper Standard issued by the National
Information Standards Organization (Z39.48–1984).

10 9 8 7 6 5 4 3 2 1

Copyright Acknowledgments

The author and publisher gratefully acknowledge permission to use portions of the following material
written by the author.

"The Concept of Surplus and the Underdeveloped Countries: Critique and Suggestions," *Review of
Radical Political Economics,* Vol. 22(2–3), pp. 215–231, 1990. Copyright, *Review of Radical Political
Economics.* Reprinted by permission of the Union for Radical Political Economics.

"Struggle for the Surplus: Jamaica, 1970–84," *METU—Studies in Development,* Vol. 6(1–2), pp.
127–152, 1989.

"The Economic Surplus: Formation, Distribution and Role in Economic Growth," *Social and Economic
Studies,* Vol. 39(1), pp. 127–152, 1990.

"Surplus and Stagnation in Jamaica: Further Notes," *Social and Economic Studies,* Vol. 41(1), pp. 45–66,
1992.

"Preferences, Technology and Population Growth in the Agricultural Household," *METU—Studies in
Development,* Vol. 19(3), pp. 289–304, 1992.

For Axel Jae-Sik

Contents

IV CONCLUDING OBSERVATIONS

Figure and Tables

Acknowledgments

Some of the results and discussions in this book have appeared in slightly different forms in professional journals. In particular, Chapter 3 is based on "The Economic Surplus and the Underdeveloped Countries: Critique and Suggestions" (*Review of Radical Political Economy*, Vol. 22: 214-230, 1990), additional information relating to Chapter 4 can be found in "Preferences, Technology and Population Growth in the Agricultural Household" (*METU— Studies in Development*, Vol. 19: 289-304, 1992) and the final part of Chapter 5 is based on "The Economic Surplus. Formation, Distribution and Role in Economic Growth" (*Social and Economic Studies*, 1990, Vol. 39: 127-152). Chapter 6 is a slightly revised version of "Surplus and Stagnation in Jamaica: Further Notes" (*Social and Economic Studies*, Vol. 41: 45-66, 1992) and parts of the analysis in Chapter 7 appear also in "Struggle for the Surplus: Jamaica, 1970-84" (*METU—Studies in Development*, Vol. 16: 127-152, 1989). The material is reprinted with permission.

I have had the opportunity of discussing various aspects of my work with a lot of people. In particular, Jim Devine, Ronald Findlay, Rajani Kanth, Victor Lippit, Mats Lundahl, Markos Mamalakis and Pan Yotopoulos have read and commented on various parts of the manuscript as have anonymous referees reading for *Social and Economic Studies*, *METU—Studies in Development* and *Economic Development and Cultural Change*. Part of the manuscript has been presented at the Third ASERCCA conference in Rome, 1987, at the 51st Americanist conference in Amsterdam, 1988, at the Eastern Economic Association meeting in New York, 1992, and at the Arne Ryde conference on *The Economic Analysis of Law* in Lund, 1993. In addition, I would like to thank SAREC, Stockholm, for a grant which financed a trip to Jamaica and the subsequent writing of Chapter 5 and the Faculty of Social Sciences at the University of Lund who granted me a three-month leave from my normal duties, which allowed me to finish the book.

I alone bear responsibility for remaining shortcomings.

I

Introduction

1

Surplus and Economic Development: An Introduction

Surplus as a concept in economics has a long history. From the Physiocrats and to the heights of classical economics manifested in the writings of David Ricardo and Karl Marx, surplus in one sense or another was at the core of the analysis. In fact, it can be argued that the very introduction of surplus into economic analysis changed the basic views of economic relations. Before the writings of Quesnay and de Mirabeau, the wealth of a nation was largely seen as a stock: the wealth of the ruler, or—for the Mercantilists—the amount of precious metals hoarded.[1] The Physiocrats' analysis changed all that. As discussed in more detail in Chapter 2, the focus of the *Tableau Économique* was on the *produit net*—output that constituted surplus in the sense that it was unnecessary for the maintenance of the current equilibrium of the economy.[2] This surplus constituted, according to the Physiocrats, the true wealth of a nation.[3] Quesnay's insight, which later proved rather fruitful, was that the wealth of a country is not a stock, an amount of resources that can be increased only at the expense of someone else's, but a flow, a share of the annual output that is not necessary for the continuation of the system. Hence, one, if not the, major contribution of the Physiocrats was to place production—if only agricultural production—at the center of economic theory.

The basic idea of surplus is very simple. If it is possible to determine the amount of resources the economic system needs to reproduce itself in subsequent periods, then it is also possible to calculate the surplus, which, of course, is simply the difference between total output and total reproduction requirements for any given period of time.

As an extremely simple illustration consider an economy in which corn is produced by labor and seed. Labor is paid a fixed wage per annum and the amount of corn sown is a fixed proportion of the number of laborers. Assume that the amount of corn needed as wages and seed to produce one unit of corn equals a. Denoting gross output of corn by Y, it follows that the amount aY is needed to produce Y. Now, if the economy is viable, that is, if the economy is able to reproduce itself, then corn output must exceed or equal corn input, that is

$$(1.1) \qquad\qquad Y \geq aY, \text{ or, } Y(1-a) \geq 0.$$

Since aY is needed to produce Y units of corn, $(1-a)Y$ is the surplus. In other words, non-negativity of the surplus is a necessary condition for viability. This is an idea that will reappear in Chapter 2.

But surplus is not only a concept of historical value. Although early neo-classicists tended to concentrate the analysis on exchange, thus pushing surplus into relative obscurity, the development of economic theory from circa 1930 and onwards has seen the development of theories focusing on surplus (albeit in a different guise). Thus for instance, Maurice Allais (1987, 697; emphasis in original) expresses the view that "*in their essence all economic operations, whatever they may be, can be thought of as boiling down to the pursuit, realization and allotment of distributable surplus.*"

Since the surplus is defined as being resources unnecessary for replication of existing economic states, it is not surprising that models or theories using that concept have focused on long-term change in the economy. In particular, the concept of surplus has been used in thinking about growth, especially with reference to underdeveloped countries. Thus for instance, Arthur Lewis (1954) defines surplus labor as the source of secular growth in dual economies; Hla Myint (1958) argues that international trade may lead to previously underutilized ("surplus") resources being incorporated into production, which in turn stimulates growth; and a number of authors, following Preobrazhensky (1965), argue that the "food surplus" being generated in the agricultural sector and transferred to non-agriculture is the key to long-term growth in underdeveloped economies.[4] None of these authors, however, define surplus in value terms: for Lewis, it is labor; for Myint, it may be all kinds of resources (the reason for the underutilization being essentially an imperfect price system); and for Preobrazhensky and his adherents, surplus is food.

Although surplus in the sense used in these writings is relatively well defined and serves a specified purpose during the course of growth, there are in the development literature frequent references to "surplus" that is not defined, but that is clearly part of the circular flow of resources and the existence of which is not necessarily due to markets being imperfect. The problem with the concept as it is used in these writings is that surplus very infrequently is given a precise definition and, when such a definition appears, its economic logic is not evident. Thus for instance, Jorge Arrate and Lucio Geller (1971, 52) define the surplus as being "the difference between the available social product and the consumption of workers and their families. The available social product is equal to the gross social product less amortisation." According to their interpretation, the size and disposal of "surplus" largely determine the faith of the economy:

> Although the economic surplus may increase as a result of tax policy, the economic surplus available for *development* in a given period will almost certainly be less than the total economic surplus, because part of the surplus will be used to finance more consumption than is strictly necessary. . . . While it is true that more rational spending on general social expenditure items is an important objective, it seems clear that, in the long run, the increase in the economic surplus available for development will occur through an increase in the total economic surplus rather than through a decrease in general social expenditures. (Arrate & Geller 1971, 53)

Although many definitions of surplus lack precise definitions or possibly have a somewhat undetermined relation to economic theory,[5] "surplus" is considered as being potentially useful and the lack of a clear, empirically meaningful definition is regarded as a deficiency in the current state of development studies. Thus, for instance, Keith Griffin (1971, 11) argues in an analysis of Latin American development: "Ideally, we would like to know—for each country—the share of the surplus in national income and the proportion of the surplus that is used productively. Unfortunately, the data for such calculations do not exist."

Paul Streeten (1971, 1008), while criticizing the concept as it is employed in Griffin's study agrees on the concept's importance: "The concept of 'economic surplus' is used frequently, without ever being clearly defined or measured. . . . [Surplus] is a useful concept and is worthy of a clearer and consistent definition."

Surplus, then, is regarded by many authors as being potentially useful for development studies. The major reason why it cannot be more frequently employed is the lack of a consistent and empirically meaningful definition.

SCOPE AND PURPOSE OF THE STUDY

Apart from this introduction and Chapter 8 in which some concluding reflections are offered, this book consists of two main parts. The first, covering Chapters 2 to 4 deals with the relation between surplus and economic growth in economic doctrines and with the issue of constructing an empirically meaningful definition of surplus.

Chapter 2 reviews theories in Classical Political Economy dealing with economic growth. In particular, the discussion revolves around the contributions of the Physiocratic school, Adam Smith and David Ricardo. Although these theories differ substantially in format as well as in content, the discussion shows that they have at least one thing in common: that the existence of a positive economic surplus is a necessary condition for economic growth.

As shall be noted subsequently, the surplus is often defined implicitly. Being the difference between total output and necessary input requirements, it follows automatically as soon as the two other concepts are defined. The Physiocratic school aside, classical theorists used the observation that there was a positive relationship between the wage rate and the rate of growth of population and were capable of defining necessary input requirements in terms of a "subsistence wage"—the wage rate at which the size of the population (and hence the size of the labor force) did neither grow nor shrink. This assumption—the Malthusian population mechanism—proved extremely fruitful since it defines the cost of labor necessary for maintaining current production.

In modern theory, the validity of the Malthusian population mechanism is less obvious and theorists have consequently been searching for a more appropriate formulation of subsistence. Chapter 3 reviews a number of post-war theories, notably those emanating from Paul Baran's formulation in *The Political Economy of Growth*, first published in 1957. Baran's approach differs markedly from those of Classical Political Economy. First, his main target is the *potential*, rather than the *actual*, surplus. Hence, Baran focuses on the difference between potential production and essential input requirements. This, in itself, is of course a perfectly respectable approach, although, as noted in Chapter 3, it is not a very useful approach when seeking to understand the functioning of actual economies: the pyramids of Egypt were not financed out of a potential surplus, nor were the Great Wall of China or the magnificent cathedrals of Europe. It was possible to erect these edifices because the economies produced a positive surplus, that is, because more was produced than was needed for maintaining the actual level of production. Keith Griffin's comment on the usefulness of the surplus concept quoted on page 5 can only be interpreted in terms of an actually existing surplus.

Surprisingly, most modern students of surplus issues have adopted the Baran approach and, with some minor modifications, continue to discuss the potential economic surplus, the most recent evidence of this is the collection of essays edited by Davis (1992). This is quite unfortunate, because the definition and estimation of the potential economic surplus is unnecessarily complicated.

The second half of Chapter 3 is devoted to the development of an empirically meaningful definition of surplus. As noted, the Baran approach— apart from dealing with the potential rather than the actual, surplus—comes equipped with a number of obscurities and inconsistencies. These include the definition of necessary input requirements, the distinction between productive and unproductive activities and the actual estimation of surplus. The method of defining and estimating the surplus in the second half of Chapter 3 is basically very simple. Taking as the point of departure the national accounting identities ensures consistency and data availability. The definition of essential input requirements—one of the major stumblingblocks in the surplus literature—is derived from the theory of dual economic development (Lewis 1954). From this, it is possible to derive a number of definitions of surplus definitions, and the final part of Chapter 3 is devoted to assess the analytical significance of these.

Chapter 4—the final chapter in Part II—discusses the agricultural surplus. The fact that the agricultural sector produces food has often given it a special place in theories of economic development. Several writers claim that the existence of a food surplus in the agricultural sector is a necessary condition for successful industrialization. Chapter 4 discusses three issues. First, a recent attempt to measure the agricultural surplus by Morrisson and Thorbecke (1990) is scrutinized and it is concluded that their approach does not add substantially to either the surplus literature or the understanding of the links between industry and agriculture in the development process. Second, a simple model is constructed which is used to analyze the formation of surplus in a pure peasant economy, that is, in an economy populated entirely by farmers. The conclusion is that farmers have control over the size as well as the composition of the surplus, which implies that any attempts on the part of the government to extract this surplus may have effects to the contrary. The final part of Chapter 4 deals with how the government can transfer surplus from the agricultural to the manufacturing sector. Several techniques are considered, including the "price scissors method" as suggested by Preobrazhensky (and adopted in a slightly modified form by Stalin), and general terms of trade manipulations. The discussion concludes, however, with Owen (1966), that the agricultural sector often carries a disproportionate tax burden, which implies that surplus is in fact transferred out of agriculture in virtually all economic systems even if the government make no conscious attempts to speed up industrialization. This, then, points to the conclusion that a more precise definition of the agricultural surplus is warranted. It seems however, that the data problems for this are, at present, insurmountable.

Part III, consisting of Chapters 5-7, applies the discussion of Part II to a case study of Jamaica, focusing in particular on the period 1972-80, although in order to put things in perspective, references are made to years both before and after this. The reason for dealing with this particular period is that Jamaica entered a deep and long recession in the early 1970s. The economy, in which real per capita income growth averaged 4.5 percent in the 1960s, shrank drastically in the 1970s reaching the bottom in 1980 when the real per capita income was only 75 percent of that a decade earlier.[6] The period 1972-80 is interesting also because during these years Jamaica was ruled by the People's National Party (PNP) headed by Michael Manley. A party with a social democratic vision, the PNP focused on social welfare and income distribution rather than production and trade. Part III asks whether the surplus approach can aid in the understanding of the causes of the deep recession.

In Chapter 5, the surplus is estimated according to the method devised in Chapter 3. Several interesting results appear. First, the surplus constitutes by far the largest component of total production and it shows an increasing trend throughout the 1970s. In the Baran framework, an increasing surplus is a sign of increasing monopoly capitalism. In this chapter, that interpretation is challenged and it is argued instead that the increasing surplus emanated from the agricultural sector being systematically disfavored. Second, the distribution of the surplus changes during the 1970s in favor of wage earners and the government at the expense of capitalists. Third, a simple test of the basic classical hypothesis of the relations between surplus and economic growth (i.e., the size of the surplus determines savings and savings determines economic growth) suggests that this mechanism was not in operation in Jamaica.

In Chapter 6, the changing distribution of the surplus is studied in more detail and an explanation of Jamaica's stagnation that fit the facts is offered. In short, the story goes as follows. The PNP government attempted to expand social services and the state's involvement in economic activities. To finance these operations, surplus extraction was intensified—in particular by putting heavier tax burdens on the shoulders of the capitalists. The expanded social services and the increased public sector benefited labor—in particular middle- and high-income earners. Since the propensity to consume import goods of these groups appears to be high, the room for capital good imports shrank drastically. Because Jamaica does not have any indigenous capital goods production, there is a clear-cut relationship between, on the one hand, the availability of foreign exchange for capital goods imports and, on the other, investments and economic growth. Hence, the Jamaican economy fell into a recession during the 1970s because (i) surplus was redistributed from high-savers (capitalists) to low-savers (middle- and high-income earners and the government) implying that savings, as share of Gross Domestic Product (GDP), fell drastically; and (ii) the increased importation of consumer goods swallowed an increasing share of the available foreign exchange, so the room for capital goods imports shrank. Hence, when the distribution of the surplus is taken into account, the classical mechanism of economic growth seems to fit the facts in Jamaica quite well. An Appendix to this chapter presents some simple regressions based on an international data set. Here as well, the classical mechanism of economic growth seems well supported, albeit a word of warning concerning the commensurability of the individual results should be issued.

Chapter 7, the final chapter in Part III, looks into the question of policy formation: why does a government pursue a particular policy? Examining the sectoral distribution of the surplus reveals that the agricultural sector seems to have been systematically disfavored (not only by the PNP government but by earlier and later governments as well). Using the little evidence that is available, it is shown that Jamaican governments have been rather responsive to the demands from interest groups and that the actual formation of policies can be explained by using an interest-group approach. If the government favors sectors, rather than groups, the economy may experience what Mamalakis (1969) denotes "sectoral clashes." The evidence is reviewed and the conclusion is drawn that the Jamaican governments seem to have favored the manufacturing sector at the expense of, in particular, the agricultural and distribution sectors. Finally, it is asked why the manufacturing sector has been favored. One possible reason could be that Jamaican governments in the 1970s still relied on what W. Arthur Lewis (1950b) called "Industrialization by Invitation", that is, that a small economy with a high labor:land ratio should concentrate on developing a viable manufacturing sector through the application of high tariffs on imported manufactured goods and generous conditions for foreign capital. Another explanation, which, it is argued in Chapter 7, seems to fit the facts quite neatly, is that surplus extraction always carries costs and that extraction from the manufacturing sector is less expensive that extraction from other sectors, for example agriculture. The apparent favorization of the manufacturing sector is thus only a chimera: the ultimate objective of the PNP government seems to have been accumulation in its own hands followed by expansion of the public sector.

Finally, Chapter 8 asks: Is Surplus Obsolete? By reviewing the discussion from Chapters 2 through 7, the answer is that the classical mechanism of economic growth still has validity and, furthermore, that the analysis suggests that the definition of surplus developed in Chapter 3 provides room for fruitful analysis of development processes.

NOTES

1. Although Petty, of course, preceded the Physiocrats by almost a century. His writings seem not, however, to have received great attention until the *Tableau Économique* had already appeared. See Walsh and Gram (1980, 14-23).

2. According to Robert Ekelund and Robert Hebert (1975, 53) one characteristic of the Physiocratic system is that "manufacturing and service industries are considered 'sterile' in the sense that they contribute nothing to the *produit net*, or net product. The net product, in turn, was looked upon as the true source of real wealth." A detailed discussion is found in Chapter 2.

3. Pasinetti (1977, 2-3). See also Spiegel (1983, 187-188) and Deane (1978, 30-31). Noteworthy in this connection is that Blaug (1978, 26), contrary to most other observers, holds the view that the *Tableau Économique* "should not be regarded as the centrepiece of the Physiocratic system." According to Robbins (1968, 8) the Physiocratic system "was a serious attempt to elucidate the circulation of wealth as defined in their system; in this respect it has some ancestral relationship to modern input-output analysis."

4. The Lewis model is further discussed in Chapters 3 and 5 and a recent formalization of Preobrazhensky's problem is presented in Chapter 4. Furthermore, the classical heritage is evident. Lewis opens his essay by the words "This essay is written in the classical tradition" and Myint is attempting to explain the pattern of trade and development in underdeveloped countries in terms of trade "models" advanced by Adam Smith. Ashok Mitra (1977, 69) holds the view that "the tradition laid down [by Rosa Luxemburg and Evgeny Preobrazhensky] has not been deviated from in any noteworthy manner in later economic writings. Even Ragnar Nurkse's discussion of the problem of capital formation in underdeveloped areas conforms to the tradition."

5. It is, for instance, not immediately clear why "the consumption of workers and their families" is deducted from net total output to yield surplus in Arrate and Geller's definition; furthermore, if the objective is to increase surplus, one possible means of doing so would be to decrease consumption of workers.

6. Calculated from IMF (1988, 440-441).

II

Theory and Measurement

2

The Role of Surplus in Classical Political Economy

What is Classical Political Economy and who were the classical economists? Different students have provided different answers. Thus, Marx (1954, 85, note 1), who seems to have coined the term, distinguished between "classical" and "vulgar" political economy, the latter "dealing with appearances only" whereas the former is theory that "since the time of W. Petty, has investigated the real relations of production in Bourgeois society." Keynes (1936, 3, note 1) used the term "classical" to denote those economists that adhered to Say's Law; that is, including even writers of the twentieth century such as Pigou but excluding the "underconsumptionists" such as Malthus, Lauderdale and Chalmers.

The most common definition of Classical Political Economy, however, seems to be that used in many recent text books on economic doctrines: Classical Political Economy is that body of theory that starts with Adam Smith (or possibly with the Physiocrats), culminates with the writings of David Ricardo (and possibly Karl Marx) and eventually was replaced by the emerging marginalist theories of the late nineteenth century. Including the Physiocrats, the period of classical theory, then, comprises approximately 115 years, from about 1756, the year of Quesnay's first article in economics, to 1871, when Menger and Jevons published their works (Walras' *Elements* was published in 1874). Although it would be possible to claim that Classical Political Economy ceased to be important long before the advent of marginalism (cf. Roll 1992, 289-310), that question need not be a concern here. The important thing for the purposes of this book is that all important theorizing in the classical period shared a number of features, in particular that the existence of "surplus" was a necessary precondition for economic growth and that only some activities (productive activities) were capable of generating surplus.

Although the discussion shall be limited to some of the most important writings of the classical period, it should be noted that the concept of surplus was part and parcel of economic theorizing long before the Physiocrats made systematic use of it. "Surplus," defined as that part of the produce that was left over after necessary production costs had been covered, was central to economics a century before the Physiocrats. Sir William Petty (1963, 43), in his *Political Arithmetick* probably written in 1672, observed: "I say, that when this man has subducted his seed out of the proceed of the harvest, and also, what himself hath both eaten and given for others in exchange for Clothes and other Natural necessities; that the remainder of Corn is the natural and true Rent of the Land for that year."

Deducting necessary expenses for the cultivator and seed from total output thus leaves the rent. Marx (1963, 357) comments on Petty's analysis: "In fact for Petty, therefore, since the value of Corn is determined by the total product minus wages and seed, rent is equal to the surplus-produce in which surplus labour is materialised. Rent here includes profit; the latter is not yet separated from rent."[1]

If Petty is interpreted to mean by "seed" the amount of corn necessary as seed to replicate this year's production next year, his analysis is very much in line with that of later classical economists. In a sense, surplus is output in excess of stationary state production. Therefore, the existence of a surplus is necessary for economic growth. It is not, however, sufficient because the surplus produce may be used either for consumption or investment. As Walter Eltis (1984, 311) succinctly has put it, "The principal proposition on which [Classical Political Economy] is based is, at the simplest, that only some economic activities generate a surplus. The reinvestment of that surplus is the main influence on the rate of economic growth."

This is the central message in Classical Political Economy (although definitions and the proposed mechanisms linking surplus to economic growth differed widely between authors). By way of illustration and in order to provide a firm base for the formulation of testable hypotheses later on, this chapter deals with three classical theories of economic growth, namely those by the Physiocrats, Adam Smith and David Ricardo.[2]

THE PHYSIOCRATIC ANALYSIS

The Physiocratic line of thought, as developed by Quesnay and de Mirabeau, is distinguished by its assertion of agriculture as the sole productive activity in the economy. Only in agriculture can output significantly exceed input. Other commodity producing activities in the economy—handicraft and the like—are in a sense supported by agriculture; they are, as shall be seen, *unproductive*, in the sense that these activities do not contribute to net output. (Spiegel 1983, 188). To appreciate the conclusions of the famed *Tableau Économique*, it is necessary to discuss in some detail the assumptions on which it is based.[3]

The Fundamental Assumptions

Quesnay's economic thinking, which culminated in several versions of the *Tableau*, was based on a firm and detailed knowledge of French agriculture. His first economic publications—two articles in Diderot's and d'Alembert's *Encyclopédie*—provided "a more detailed account of the agriculture of the time than the work of any other great classical economist" (Eltis 1984, 1). There are several important assumptions. First, Quesnay distinguishes three agricultural techniques of production: cultivation by labor alone, cultivation with ox-drawn ploughs and cultivation with horse-drawn ploughs. When farming takes place with only labor, production is small and barely sufficient for survival: "A poor man who only draws from his land by his labour produce of little value such as potatoes, buckwheat, chestnuts, etc., who feeds himself on them, who buys nothing and sells nothing, works only for himself: he lives in wretchedness, and he and the land he tills brings nothing to the state."[4]

No part of his produce can be extracted as taxes and he cannot afford to pay rent. Consequently, the laborer who tills the soil without oxen or horses does not produce a surplus. As for cultivation with oxen or horses, production of a surplus is possible. Here, Quesnay notes that cultivation with horses is possible only for wealthy farmers because "a farmer who sets himself up with a four-horse plough must incur considerable expenditure before he obtains his first crop."[5] Where wealthy farmers are not available, landlords may have their land tilled by *métayers* with oxen in return for half of the produce. Hence, the existence of rich farmers is a necessary precondition for *la grande culture*, based on horses; without such farmers landlords are forced to resort to *la petite culture*, using oxen under the *métayer* system.

Production is much higher in *la grande culture*, mainly because the land that the oxen need for pasture in *la petite culture* may profitably be used to stock other animals such as sheep, beef cattle and pigs. Quesnay compares profitability in the two systems, demonstrating that the *produit net* (the excess of output over the annual costs of production) in *la petite culture* is 36 percent, whereas in *la grande culture* it is close to 100 percent.

The second assumption is that the size of the surplus is dependent on the capital intensity in production. Capital comes in three forms: *avances fonciéres*, initial expenditures on clearing, building and the like; *avances annuelles*, current expenditures on raw material, wages and seed; and *avances primitives*, expenditures on equipment, including cattle and maintenance (Schumpeter 1954, 236). Quesnay makes detailed comparisons between the rates of return on capital in the two systems and concludes that although the return on total capital in *la petite culture* is some 12 percent, the same return in *la grande culture* may be as high as 20 percent (see Eltis 1975a, 170-173). Expansion of agriculture is limited by the availability of capital and entrepreneurs; land and labor are not scarce. The fact that the availability of wealthy farmers is limited is also the reason why *la grande culture*—which unquestionably is the most profitable technique—does not drive *la petite culture* out of existence.

The third assumption is that agriculture is the only activity capable of producing a surplus. This assumption, as Eltis (1975a, 176) correctly notes, is not very strange—despite the fact that Quesnay's use of the word "sterile" to characterize the manufacturing sector prevented many later economists to attach any importance to Physiocratic theory. The manufacturing sector is "sterile" in the sense that the value of production equals cost of production; in modern terminology there are no super-normal profits. If markets for manufactures are characterized by perfect competition (*concurrence libre*), all super-normal profits disappear. However, in agriculture it is, according to Quesnay, possible to produce a surplus above wages and normal profits. The reason is that Quesnay makes the assumption used by the classical English economists: costs in agriculture are fixed in terms of food. Given that payment to farm laborers is made in food and that the long-run level of this wage is set according to subsistence needs, any increase in cultivation efficiency necessarily increases output relatively to costs. This surplus is appropriated by the landlord, the Church or the King by virtue of society's institutions, in particular the limitation of land ownership to the nobility.

The fourth important assumption made by Quesnay is that the effective demand for marketed output depends on the expenditure of the recipients of the surplus (i.e., landlords, the Church and the King):

> The works of agriculture make good their expenses, repay the costs of work, procure incomes for the workers; and in addition produce the revenues of the estates. Those who buy industrial goods pay for the costs, and the workmanship, and the merchant's return; but these goods produce no income beyond this.
>
> Thus all the expenditure on the works of industry only drawn revenue from landed income; for works that do not generate revenue can only exist through the wealth of those who pay for them.[6]

In addition, it is important that the surplus recipients continue to spend their income. Quesnay goes on to show, in the first version of the *Tableau*, how the spending of the surplus income affects both demand for manufacturing and agricultural goods and how a multiplier is working, the size of the multiplier being determined by the fraction of surplus income that is spent on agricultural goods (Eltis 1984, 34-38). The spending pattern of the surplus recipients is, as shall be seen, instrumental to economic growth. This is an idea that will reappear in the writings of the English classical economists.

The preceding discussion paves the road for three of the Physiocrats' important conclusions. First, a case was constructed for a single tax—*l' impôt unique*—that was to be levied on the *produit net*. Second, the agricultural activities formed the backbone of the economy: without an expanding agricultural sector, the rest of the economy would stagnate or recede. Third, the "sterile" sector (manufacturing) was dependent on the "productive" sector (agriculture) both because a market for manufacturing goods was created through the production and extraction of a *produit net* and because the agricultural sector supplied inputs to the manufacturing sector. However, the agricultural sector was completely independent of the manufacturing sector.

The *Tableau Économique* and the Theory of Growth

The activities of Quesnay and Victor de Riquetti, Marquis de Mirabeau formed a school originally known as *les économistes*. The disciples—including Mercier de la Rivière, Le Trosne and Baudeau—showed, according to Schumpeter (1954, 223) a faithfulness to Quesnay's teaching "for which there are but two analogues in the whole history of economics: the fidelity of the orthodox Marxists to the message of Marx and the fidelity of the orthodox Keynesians to the message of Keynes." Quesnay's theory of economic growth starts from a *Tableau* in stationary equilibrium and different parameters—the propensity to consume, the rate and form of taxation—of this *Tableau* are then changed in order to ascertain their effects on economic expansion.

The Stationary State. Assume an economy in which the agricultural sector generates a *produit net* equal to R. This is appropriated in its entirety by the landlords who spend a proportion q on food and $(1 - q)$ on manufactures. Assume further that all workers, in both the sterile and productive sectors, show the same spending pattern, q from the productive sector and $(1 - q)$ from the sterile sector.

In the first round, the productive sector sells food worth qR to the landlords and the sterile sector sells $(1 - q)R$ worth of manufactures. In the next round, farmers spend a proportion $(1 - q)$ of their income (qR) on purchases from the sterile sector and the workers in the sterile sector spend $q(1 - q)R$ on food from the productive sector. Denoting the productive sector's total purchases by X_p and the sterile sector's total purchases by X_s, results in

$$(2.1) \qquad X_p = R\left(\frac{2q - q^2}{1 - q + q^2}\right) \qquad\qquad X_s = R\left(\frac{1 - q^2}{1 - q + q^2}\right).$$

By way of example, assume that the value of production in the productive sector is 2,000 livres, that $R = 1,000$ livres (so the rate of return on annual advances is 100 percent as in *la grande culture*), that the value of production in the sterile sector is 1,000 livres and that $q = 0.5$. Using these figures in (2.1) gives $X_p = 1,000$ and $X_s = 1,000$. Since the purchases made by the sectors are input for production, both sectors show production costs equal to 1,000 livres.

Production costs in the sterile sector equal value of output, whereas value of output in the productive sector exceeds production costs. The difference between value of output and cost of production in the productive sector is the *produit net*, in this case equal to 1,000 livres.

Initially each sector received 500 livres from the landlords (continuing the numerical example) and total spending was 1,000 lives in each sector. Hence, a multiplier is in action; in this example it is equal to 2. In fact, a q equal to 0.5 gives the maximum multiplier; it approaches 1 as q approaches either 0 or 1.

This is a stationary state: the economy can reproduce itself as long as no parameters change. However, several important assumptions must be maintained for this to happen. In particular, all receipts are immediately spent and no money are spent abroad, that is, there is no international trade (Eltis 1984, 20).

As can be seen from (2.1), the revenue to each sector is completely determined by two factors: the size of the *produit net*, R, and the propensity to consume goods from the productive sector, q. Note in particular that whereas q determines the relative size of the two sectors, R in effect determines the level of effective demand.[7] However, the stationary state demonstrated by Quesnay in the first *Tableau* from 1758-59 is not very general: the stationary state attained requires several restricting assumptions:

> Thus the equilibrium of the *Tableau* depends partly on the fact that a multiplier of *two* can be applied to the Revenue to ascertain its effects on aggregate market demand, and the same multiplier of *two* is applied to what agriculture receives because of the proposition that agricultural outputs are twice agricultural inputs. Thus the multiplier involved in the expenditure of the revenue is the same as the multiplier of the soil, for it is only in these conditions that each class will get back at the end of a year what it had at the beginning. (Eltis 1984, 24, emphasis in original)

Economic Growth in the Tableau. Finally—following Eltis (1984, 42-49)— the examination turns to the effects of a q that is not equal to 0.5. It will be recalled from the earlier discussion (see page 17) that an expanding agricultural sector is necessary for growth in the economy. It will prove instructive to give two examples—one in which $q > 0.5$ and one in which $q < 0.5$—to show that the *Tableau* does not produce symmetrical effects; the sterile sector is dependent on the productive but not vice versa.

Recall the mechanics of the model. The *produit net* is appropriated by landlords and part of it goes back to the productive sector in the form of *avances annuelles* and part goes to the sterile sector in exchange for manufacturing goods. The recipients of this revenue use part of it to purchase goods from the other sector. Thus if the *produit net* is 1,000 livres and the rate of return on agricultural advances is 100 percent, farmers receive, through the period under consideration, 1,000 livres from the circulation of the revenue as discussed and—if $q = 0.5$—500 livres from the sterile sector in return for inputs. The farmers use these 1,500 livres for two purposes: to buy industrial products (and given that $q = 0.5$, this cost them 500 livres) and to pay rent, which is 1,000 livres. The revenues received by the productive sector are thus exactly sufficient for that sector's expenditures. Hence, $q = 0.5$ represents in this case a stationary state.

Assume now that, from this equilibrium, q falls to 0.4. As can be seen from (2.1), farmers' receipts fall to 842 livres, whereas manufacturers' receipts increase to 1,105 livres. In the next round, the farmers receive 442 livres from the sterile sector in return for inputs and spend 60 percent of their 842 livres on manufactures. Hence, the productive sector receives 1,284 livres and it spends 1,505 livres (1,000 on rent and 505 on manufactures). Hence, a larger share of the harvest has been allocated to the manufacturing sector than before, and agricultural advances are about 5.5 percent lower. In further periods, the smaller agricultural advances lead to a smaller harvest and the reduction in rent leads to lower demand for both food and manufactures. Even though the increased revenue to the sterile sector increases the output of manufactures, the demand for manufactures diminishes—because both landlords and farmers demand less. In this example, the revenues to the sterile sector fall to less than 500 livres after three years (see Eltis 1975b, 329-335, for details).

Now, compare this to a situation where q increases from 0.5 to 0.6. Here, agricultural advances increase from 1,000 to 1,042 livres. Advances to the sterile sector are reduced from 500 to 421 livres since q has increased. However, since revenues in the productive sector increases rent increases, so demand for manufactures (and hence revenues in the sterile sector) increases after an initial drop. In this example, when annual advances to agriculture increase by approximately 4.2 percent per annum, it takes five years for the sterile sector's advances to get back to 500 livres and it continues to increase from that point (Eltis 1984, 46). The rate of growth of agricultural advances (and therefore the rate of growth of the entire economy) depends entirely on q, and the calculations of Eltis (1984, 47) suggest that the maximum rate of growth is attained at $q = 0.749$, giving a rate of growth of agricultural advances of approximately 6.73 percent per annum. Hence, growth in the sterile sector is dependent on growth in the productive sector since it is, in effect, the rate of growth of *effective demand* in the latter that determines the rate of growth of the former. In this sense, the manufacturing sector is dependent on the agricultural sector, but not vice versa.

In conclusion, the Physiocratic model, represented by the *Tableau Économique*, shows how two factors determine the fate of the economy: the amount of output that is not necessary for maintenance of the current level of production (i.e. the size of the surplus, here represented by the *produit net*) and the consumption behavior of those in command of that surplus. As shall be seen, this idea is central in classical theory.

ADAM SMITH'S THEORY OF GROWTH

During his stay in France, Adam Smith became acquainted with the Physiocratic school (Walsh and Gram 1980, 58-61). He found it to be "the nearest approximation to the truth that has yet been published upon the subject of political economy" (Smith 1976, IV.ix.38). He was, however, not content with the assumption of agriculture being the only productive activity: "The capital error of ... [the Physiocratic] system, however, seems to lie in its representing the class of artificers, manufacturers and merchants, as altogether barren and unproductive" (Smith 1976, IV.ix.29). Consequently, one of Smith's major alterations were to assume that virtually all economic activities *could* generate a surplus. As shall be seen, however, the major conclusions of the Physiocrats' analysis with regard to economic growth were not changed by Smith's alterations.

Smith's version of the process of economic growth is complex and difficult to formalize. It seems, however, as if Smith emphasizes two determinants of the rate of growth: continuous and increasing division of labor and the accumulation of capital: "The crucial requirements for growth ... were that there should be increasing subdivision of labour, raising average productivity, and that savings out of profits should be more than enough to maintain existing capital" (Deane 1978, 33). A "pure" model, in Hicks' (1965, 37-38) terminology, of Smith's growth process may look like the following.[8]

Assume that the only activity in the economy is corn production. It is produced by labor and seed, used in fixed proportions. Wages are paid in corn and in advance out of the previous period's output. Denoting the wage plus the amount of seed used per man by w, it follows that the maximum employment possible in period t is

$$(2.2) \qquad\qquad L_t = X_{t-1}/w$$

where X is total production and L number of laborers.

This is a maximum, since capitalists can choose to use their produce for other things than expansion of corn production. Assume for the moment that capitalists do not consume but spend their entire income on expansion of corn production so (2.2) is satisfied. Denote average labor productivity by p (so $p_t = X_t/L_t$) and assume that p does not change over time. Output in period t, then, equals

$$(2.3) \qquad\qquad X_t = pL_t = (p/w)X_{t-1}.$$

Define "surplus," S, as the amount of corn that does not accrue to workers as wages:

(2.4) $$S_t = X_t - wL_t = (p - w)L_t.$$

From (2.2) and (2.3), it follows that the rate of growth, g, equals

(2.5) $$g_t = (X_t - X_{t-1})/X_{t-1} = (p/w) - 1.$$

Noting that "the rate of surplus," s, equals

(2.6) $$s_t = S_t/X_t = 1 - (w/p),$$

the rate of growth can be expressed as a function of the distribution of the produce between surplus and wages:

(2.7) $$g_t = \sigma_t/w,$$

where σ_t is surplus per worker, S_t/L_t.

Now, in a more general fashion assume that capitalists use a constant share k ($0 \leq k \leq 1$) of total income from the previous period for expansion of corn production; $(1 - k)$ is used unproductively.[9] Since total production in any period consists of wages and seed (W) plus surplus (S), employment is positively related to k. The wage fund in period t equals

(2.8) $$W_t = k(W_{t-1} + S_{t-1}).$$

Following the same line of reasoning, it is easy to see that the rate of growth is now equal to $k(p/w) - 1$. To see how growth depends on the surplus, observe that the rate of surplus per worker is $\sigma_t = p - w$. Defining "the rate of productive surplus" as the amount of the increment of output that will be allocated to the wage fund in the subsequent period, that is, as $\alpha = kp - w$, and keeping k, p and w constant the rate of growth when $k \leq 1$ equals

(2.9) $$g = \alpha/w.$$

From (2.9) it can be seen that the rate of growth is determined by two factors: first, the "rate of productive surplus," that is, the difference between the produce reserved for investment in corn production and the cost of labor, and second, the share of the surplus allocated to productive (i.e., surplus yielding) investments (reflected in k).

So it can be seen that the rate and disposal of the surplus are as important for the rate of growth in Smith's system as they are for the Physiocrats. In fact, Smith repeatedly states that frugality is a virtue and that a lavish government represents a danger to society. Since unproductive consumption stands in opposition to accumulation "every prodigal appears to be a publick enemy and every frugal man a benefactor" (Smith 1976, II.iii.25). And further, "Both productive and unproductive labour, and those who do not labour at all, are all equally maintained by the annual produce of the land and labour of the country . . . According, therefore, as a smaller or greater proportion of it is in any one year employed in maintaining unproductive hands, the more in the one case and the less in the other will remain for the productive, and the next year's produce will be greater or smaller accordingly." (Smith 1976, II.iii.3)

Smith's analysis of growth differs considerably from that of the Physiocrats, but in one important respect they are similar. It is the conclusion that the main influences on the rate of growth are the size and disposal of the surplus.

RICARDO'S THEORY

David Ricardo is sometimes considered the chief theorist among classical economists. First and foremost, his contribution is said to be the theory of distribution.[10] It is important, however, to realize that the Ricardian theory of distribution is developed against the background of a theory of growth; Ricardo analyzes "the natural course of rent, profit, and wages" (Ricardo 1951, 5). His integrated theory of growth and distribution is best exposed by the aid of a diagram.[11]

In the upper panel of Figure 2.1, APL is the average product of labor and MPL the marginal product of labor. The long-run wage, w, is determined by the reproduction cost of labor. Land is of varying quality, implying that landlords owning intra-marginal units of land are able to extract part of the output as rent. Owners of marginal units, however, do not receive rent; the marginal product is divided between wages and profit. Landlords thus extract a rent equal to the difference between output on intra-marginal lands and output on marginal lands. In Figure 2.1, therefore, with L0 workers employed, total output (0ABL0) is divided between rent (ABDC), profits (CDEw) and wages (wEL00).

Economic growth in this system is attained by capitalists investing their profits and thus expanding production. The simplest case (which is the one considered here) is characterized by the absence of fixed capital. "Investment of profits" thus means additions to the wage fund. Expansion of the wage fund implies growth of the demand for labor, which temporarily increases wages. The Malthusian population mechanism, however, ensures that growth of population responds to changing wages, so increased supply on the labor market will eventually press wages back to w. Due to diminishing returns in agriculture, the economy is eventually forced into stagnation. This is illustrated in the lower half of Figure 2.1.

The curve OT measures net-of-rent production and OS total wages. The vertical difference between OT and OS thus measures total profits. At

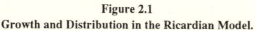

Figure 2.1
Growth and Distribution in the Ricardian Model.

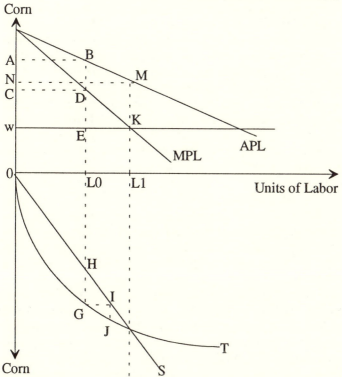

employment L0, workers receive HL0 wages and capitalists GH profits. As previously noted, investment of profits creates a temporary increase of wages. As population growth presses wages back toward w, employment increases. In the lower half of Figure 2.1 the economy thus follows the HGIJ path. Profits decline due to diminishing returns and wages will eventually constitute the entire net-of-rent product. In the figure, this occurs at employment L1. In Figure 2.1, the "natural" wage, w, equals the marginal product of labor at L1, so total production is divided between wages (wKL10) and rent (NMKw). Because it is assumed that landlords consume their income, the only source of accumulation is profits; hence the incentive to invest disappears with profits and the economy has stagnated.

Which are the determinants of growth and what is the significance of the surplus in Ricardo's model? First, growth is determined by the amount invested in each period. Ricardo uses a wage fund theory of employment, so it is the expansion of variable capital that determines the expansion of employment and output. Because the long run wage equals labor's reproduction cost, wages are entirely consumed. Because it is assumed that landlords use their income for a "riotous living," capitalists are the only savers, and the rate of expansion is directly related to the amount of profits saved.

Second, it is assumed that the marginal propensity to save out of profits is constant. Hence variations in the volume of profits do not affect the rate of savings. Necessary costs of production, therefore, are the cost of wages and the remainder is surplus.[12] Economic rent is necessary to call forth land, and profits are necessary to call forth investable capital, but these costs, economically necessary as they are, represent a surplus in the sense that capitalists' incomes are not necessary for their living in the same sense as wages are necessary for the subsistence of laborers; they are essential for capitalists' accumulation, but not for their bare survival.

Third, the assumption that only capitalists save is a simplifying one: stagnation occurs even if it is assumed that landlords save as well. To see this, follow Dasgupta (1985, 32) and assume that the ownership of land is transferred to capitalists. Since the urge to accumulate is derived from the capitalists' search for new profits, nothing has changed (except that the capitalists now "live like gentlemen"). Surplus is a necessary, not a sufficient, condition for economic growth.

Finally, although the assumption that landlords do not save is irrelevant to the pattern of growth, the rate of economic expansion is dependent on the disposal of the surplus. The addition to the wage fund (i.e., accumulation) depends on the capitalists' propensity to save: the higher that propensity, the higher the rate of growth: "The additional wage fund ... available at the beginning of a production period depends upon total profits in the previous period and the propensity for capitalists to 'save' out of profits" (Dasgupta 1985, 28). If the stationary state can be postponed by, for instance, continuous technical progress (which, in Figure 2.1, would shift APL and MPL outward, and OT clockwise), the rate of growth depends on the consumption behavior of the capitalists.

As far as the surplus is concerned, Ricardo reaches a conclusion similar to that of earlier classical economists: economic growth depends on the size and disposition of the surplus.

So far, the concept of "surplus" has been shown to occupy a central position in the classical theory of growth. This theory has become somewhat out of fashion, but, as Walter Eltis (1984, 337) has remarked, "there are no logical weaknesses in the classical theory of economic growth, and like all good economics, it is valid where its assumptions hold." Two factors are central in the classical theory of economic growth: the size of the surplus and how it is disposed of. The size of the surplus partly depends on surplus disposal, that is, on whether it is used for consumption or saving and investment, but also on the fact that only some activities actually can generate a surplus. Frequent references have already been made to the distinction between "productive" and "unproductive" activities and we have seen that these concepts appear to be an important part of Classical Political Economy. It is now time to discuss these concepts in more detail.

PRODUCTIVE AND UNPRODUCTIVE ACTIVITIES
IN CLASSICAL ANALYSIS

In the famous chapter entitled "Of the accumulation of Capital, or of productive and unproductive Labour" Adam Smith (1976, II.iii) analyzes the situation in which only some activities may lead to economic growth. He provides, in half a page, three definitions that are not necessarily mutually consistent:

> There is one sort of labour which adds to the value of the subject upon which it is bestowed: There is another which has no such effect. The former, as it produces a value, may be called productive; the latter, unproductive labour. Thus, the labour of a manufacturer adds, generally, to the value of the materials which he works upon, that of his own maintenance, and of his master's profit . . . The labour of the menial servant, on the contrary, does not fix or realize itself in any particular subject or vendible commodity. His services generally perish in the very instant of their performance, and seldom leave any trace or value behind them, for which an equal quantity of service could afterwards be procured. (Smith 1976, II.iii.1)

Productive labor adds value to what is produced; unproductive labor does not. Productive labor increases profits; unproductive labor does not. Finally, productive labor is said to result in material goods, whereas unproductive labor result in services. It is clear that these definitions may conflict: for instance, the producer of services may well make profits; or a commodity's value may increase when labor is added without increasing profits. Although Smith himself seems to use the third definition—the one that identifies unproductive labor with the production of services—it is in fact the second one—where productive labor produces a profit—that carries on the tradition from the mercantilist and Physiocratic tradition (Roll 1992, 150-151).

As previously shown, the Physiocrats defines productive activities as those in which it is possible to produce a surplus, that is, activities in which value of output exceeds cost of production. Productive labor in the Physiocratic tradition, then, is labor that is employed in the agricultural sector.[13] Similarly, early English economists seem to have viewed the generation of a surplus—in the form of rent or profits—as characteristic for productive activities (cf. the quotation from Petty on page 14).

The exact definition of productive and unproductive is largely a matter of taste and the issues at hand; the important thing—and this question is returned to in Chapter 3—is that a distinction is made between activities that can add to economic growth and those that cannot. It is equally important to realize that unproductive activities are not necessarily undesirable. According to Smith (1976, II.iii.2), unproductive labor include "the sovereign, . . . ,with all the officers both of justice and war who serve under him, his whole army and navy [and also] some of the most frivolous professions: churchmen, lawyers, physicians, men of letters of all kinds; players, bufoons, musicians, opera-singers, opera-dancers, &c."

The importance of making a distinction between productive and unproductive activities becomes clear when we analyze Ricardo's theory of growth. Recall from the preceding (page 22 and onwards) that the result of production is divided between laborers, capitalists and landlords. In a sense, only wages are necessary costs of production: since workers live on a subsistence minimum due to the Malthusian population check, wages must be forthcoming to ensure that the working force survive until the next production period. Profits and rent, however, are not necessary for the continuation of production—unless the analysis is made somewhat less abstract and a minimum rate of profit below which capital for expansion of production would not be forthcoming is postulated. In this sense, then, profits and rents are surplus incomes: they are not necessary for the continuation of production. They accrue to capitalists and landlords, respectively, by virtue of property rights and control of the means of production.

In the simplest Ricardian model, capitalists use their entire income to expand production and landlords use their entire production for consumption— of goods and services. As long as it is assumed, along with Ricardo, that Say's Law holds, capitalists accumulate their profits, putting it to work again, whereas landlords are parasites who benefit from the toil of labor simply because they possess land and who expedite the economy's inevitable travel toward stagnation because they prefer prodigality in consumption to accumulation.

Here, again, is the essence of the classical mechanism of economic growth. Surplus is produced by the employment of productive labor and the behavior of the recipients of the surplus determines whether or not economic growth can continue. For Ricardo, the capitalists are the heroes of society, because they engage in *productive consumption*, putting more productive laborers to work. Landlords, on the other hand, engage in *unproductive consumption*, hiring servants and building mansions.[14]

The distinction between productive and unproductive activities is thus central in the analysis of the links between surplus and economic growth. As seen in Chapter 3, however, this distinction is not unproblematic and it is quite simple to slip into the trap of juxtaposing unproductive and undesirable. It will be argued in Chapter 3, however, that the Smithian distinction between those activities that produce a surplus and those that do not is vital to the analysis of the causes of economic growth.

CONCLUDING REMARKS

This chapter has dealt with the theory of growth in Classical Political Economy. In this collection of theories, although complex and diverse, three features stand out as unifying. First is the assumption that it is possible to identify a surplus, defined as output that is not necessary for maintaining production at the current level and that this surplus is a necessary precondition for economic growth. Second is that only some activities are capable of generating a surplus; these are denoted "productive." Third is that the surplus can be disposed of in different ways only some of which are conducive for economic growth.

Although the theory and its assumptions were replaced in the late nineteenth century by marginalist theories emphasizing the allocation of given resources, it is important to realize that theories founded on classical thinking are not necessarily obsolete. The idea that the resources in the economy enter a circular flow, that markets are interlinked and that resources are not "given" but determined by the historical performance of the economy is still viable. Furthermore, it is important to recall that classical economists were all development economists, studying developing countries (in particular, Britain; cf. Bardhan 1993). This makes it difficult to escape the idea that the classical theory of economic growth with its assumptions on social classes, population growth and the like still has some relevance for developing countries.

The application of classical theory to the problems of today's developing countries requires a number of problems to be solved of which one is definitional: how should the concepts "subsistence" and "surplus" be given meaningful definitions and how should they be statistically interpreted? These issues are addressed in Chapter 3.

NOTES

1. Incidentally, a more appealing definition of Classical Political Economy might start with Petty, whom Marx appoints founder of political economy (cf. Roll, 1992, 85).

2. The Marxian approach is not discussed here. As will become evident in Chapter 3, the definition of surplus provided in this book is less suitable to the Marxian approach to "surplus value."

3. This discussion is based on that in Eltis (1984, Ch. 1). See also Walsh and Gram (1980, 28-32), Deane (1978, 30-31) and Samuelson (1982).

4. *François Quesnay et la Physiocratie*, Institut National d'Etudes Démographiques, Paris, 1958, p. 498 (ed. by L. Salleron). Quoted in Eltis (1984, 5).

5. Ibid.

6. Ibid. Quoted in Eltis (1984, 15).

7. It has been suggested by several students (e.g. Meek 1962, 269; Schumpeter 1954, 240; Foley 1973) that Quesnay, the physician, got the original idea of the circulation of money and goods in the economy by analogy to the circulation of blood, discovered by William Harvey in 1628. Quesnay was involved in a long dispute between physicians and surgeons from 1730 onwards and he wrote several studies on the circulation of blood, in particular *Traité des effets et de l'usage de la saignée*. Compare Foley (1973, 123-125).

8. See also Dasgupta (1985, 24-26).

9. That is, in period t a share k of total income generated in $t — 1$ is used as a wage fund.

10. "Ricardo thus approached the study of general economics as a student of distribution, a shift in emphasis from Adam Smith who had placed the problem of production in the center" (Spiegel 1983, 319); see also O'Brien (1975, 214).

11. Similar figures appear in Kaldor (1960, 212) and Baumol (1959, 19). A mathematical treatment is provided by Pasinetti (1960).

12. It would of course be possible to specify a minimum rate of profit below which capitalists' savings cease to come forward. In this case, it would seem relevant to define surplus as total value of output less subsistence wages less that minimum volume of profits. See Caravale and Tosato (1980) for different specifications of Ricardo's model.

13. Although, as was noted on page 15, some agricultural labor may be unproductive in the sense that they do not produce a surplus over and above what is necessary for bare survival. This refers, of course, to labor that tills the soil without help from oxen or horses.

14. The distinction between productive and unproductive consumption is interesting and focuses on whether the outlay of surplus income increases the employment of productive labour. In the long exchange between Ricardo and Malthus regarding the possibility of "general gluts," the distinction is central because Malthus uses it to argue that the very fact that landlords engage in unproductive consumption saves the economy from overproduction. For a fuller discussion, see Roll (1992, 180-189) or Bleany (1976). Ricardo's argument that the employment of servants does not increase productive employment can be questioned on the ground that servants are likely to spend their wages on food and other necessities, so their employment contributes indirectly to productive employment. On this point, see the erudite study by Helen Boss (1990, esp. Ch. 4).

3

Making Surplus Visible: A National Accounts Approach

It was demonstrated in Chapter 2 how the concept of surplus was used in Classical Political Economy and it was suggested that the concept may prove useful for analyzing the causes of economic growth. This chapter[1] examines some recent attempts to construct a measure of the surplus, and an alternative method of measuring surplus is developed. The "surplus approach"[2] utilizes mainly national accounts. A number of studies, to which references are given in the following, have attempted to construct measures of the economic surplus. Without exception, these studies have relied on material not generally available for underdeveloped countries—such as information on the number of pure rentiers in rural areas. These studies may have their merits, but it is rather difficult to render them comparable to other studies or to repeat them for different time periods. The major advantages of relying on national accounts are, first, that such statistics are often compiled according to the United Nations' Systems of National Accounts (SNA), thus making international comparisons possible and, second, that national accounts are published rather regularly, thus making it possible to study the development of the surplus over time (which, typically, is impossible using the "rare data" method).

Since the publication in 1957 of Paul Baran's *The Political Economy of Growth*, a number of studies have attempted to operationalize the hypotheses and test the propositions generated in this and the companion volume by Baran and Paul Sweezy (1966). In particular, the attempts have been to produce an operationable definition of "surplus." This is an important subject, both because Baran's hypotheses are sufficiently interesting and provoking to deserve close scrutiny and because—as was argued in Chapter 2—surplus as an analytical concept may assist in the analysis of the causes and cures of underdevelopment. As will be argued, however, neither Baran's nor the other studies' surplus concepts are very useful for empirical analysis.

THE CONCEPT OF SURPLUS

In *The Political Economy of Growth*, Paul Baran develops three different versions of the surplus:

1. *The actual economic surplus*, equal to the difference between current production and current consumption.
2. *The potential economic surplus*, equal to potential production less essential consumption. This surplus exists in four distinct forms: luxury consumption, output lost because of the employment of unproductive workers, output lost because of the "irrationality and wastefulness of the prevailing economic organization" and finally output forgone owing to the existence of unemployment "caused primarily by the anarchy of capitalist production and the deficiency of efficient demand" (Baran 1957, 24).
3. *The planned economic surplus*, which is "the difference between society's 'optimum' output attainable ... under conditions of planned 'optimal' utilization of all productive resources—and some chosen 'optimum' volume of consumption" (Baran 1957, 279).

As Victor Lippit (1985) points out, Baran's contribution lies in the identification of the potential economic surplus; because the actual economic surplus equals current savings and the planned economic surplus equals planned investment under socialism, and there is not much point in renaming known concepts.

Although the potential economic surplus contains a number of flaws,[3] these can quite easily be corrected. What is more important is that the very foundation on which the concept is erected can be questioned. Furthermore, recent attempts to operationalize surplus take as their point of departure Baran's categorization; hence, the foundation of these as well is questionable.[4]

There are two crucial issues, both of which are dealt inadequately with by Baran. First is the definition of "essential consumption" and its relation to "subsistence." Second is the division of the labor force into its "productive" and "unproductive" parts. To some extent, these problems are inherited by Baran's followers; the following critique thus apply to these as well.

The Definition of Subsistence

As noted in Chapter 2, in Classical Political Economy essential consumption was defined as the volume of consumption that is allowed by the natural wage. And, according to Ricardo (1951, 93), "the natural price of labour is that price which is necessary to enable the labourers, one with another, to subsist and to perpetuate their race, without either increase or diminution." From this it follows, of course, that in the long run consumption out of wages is equal to essential consumption, provided that the Malthusian population mechanism is working, that is, provided that the labor force increases more rapidly than the demand for labor if market wages exceed the "natural" wage.

"Surplus" in general equals "output" less "subsistence," where the latter term is the amount of resources necessary for the maintenance of the system. This is why the natural wage in Ricardo's system is equal to subsistence: it is the wage that enables laborers to subsist. Whether "subsistence" is economically, socially, culturally or physiologically determined is a debated issue.[5]

Baran (1957, 30) defines essential consumption as "the amount and composition of real income necessary for what is socially considered as necessary." And he clarifies: "Where living standards are in general low—and the basket of goods available to the consumer little variegated—essential consumption can be circumscribed in terms of calories, other nutrients, quantities of clothing, fuel, dwelling space, etc. Even where the level of consumption is relatively high and involves a large variety of consumer goods and services, a judgement of the amount of real income necessary for what is socially considered a 'decent livelihood' can be made" (Baran 1970, 276-277).

Things are not as unproblematic as Baran suggests here. First, who decides what is a "decent livelihood"? This is a central issue, since the availability of regularly published data is a prerequisite for long-term studies. In Baran's view, estimates from official authorities such as the United Nations' Food and Agriculture Organization or the Bureau of Labor Statistics can be used. Alternatively, estimates of subsistence may be carried out by the researcher, because the concept of decent livelihood is "wholly accessible to scientific inquiry and to rational judgement." Although Baran's statement that it is possible to calculate subsistence requirements should not be disputed, it is important to keep in mind the difficulties involved in estimating subsistence requirements for a long period of time or making such figures internationally commensurable. Given the present state of data quality, Baran's definition of subsistence requirements encourages neither the study of the relations between surplus and long-term growth nor the international comparisons of surplus patterns.

The second problem is that Baran earmarks part of output for "subsistence consumption." Subsistence per worker is defined, and it is postulated that subsistence consumption (i.e., subsistence per worker multiplied by the number of workers) should be deducted from output in order to calculate surplus. Similar procedures are adopted by Lippit (1985, 12-13) and Stanfield (1974, 70-72). The implications of this procedure are examined here in the light of actual versus potential surplus.

Carl Riskin's (1975) definition of essential consumption is slightly different: he assumes that the wage equals the value of essential consumption.

This has severe implications. If real wages across sectors are not equal, different labor categories have different essential consumption. In most modern societies, Riskin's definition would imply for instance that a professor of economics would have a higher *essential* consumption than, for example, a farmer. The logic behind such an assumption is not immediately clear. As is argued later, irrespective of whether "subsistence" is assumed to be culturally, physiologically or socially determined, the appropriate procedure is to have one and the same subsistence basket for all individuals.[6]

In his book *The Economic Surplus and Neo-Marxism*, Ron Stanfield (1973) attempts to estimate the surplus as defined by Baran. To measure what is denoted "personal essential consumption" he uses the City Workers' Family Budget compiled by the U.S. Bureau of Labor Statistics. "Aside from the convenience involved in its availability and its methodological scope," writes Stanfield (1973, 13), "this budget seems to reflect the spirit of the subsistence minimum as defined in the writings of Ricardo, Marx and Baran, if allowance is made for the degree of civilization of the United States." Although it seems clear that Stanfield's definition comes close to Baran's, it is doubtful whether it could be used for underdeveloped countries or, indeed, for international comparisons of the relations between the size and composition of the surplus and, say, the pattern of economic growth. Apart from the general deficiencies in Baran's concept as have been pointed out, Stanfield's definitions come equipped with two possible weak points. First is the data material. It is compiled by the Bureau of Labor Statistics and includes the costs for a family of four living at a "modest but adequate" level. Stanfield's (1973, 11) discussion illustrates very well the point made here: that such data are not published with regular intervals and that the data is subject to constant revisions. The point here is not to argue that Stanfield's investigation is erroneous, but rather that the methodology devised can hardly be applied outside the United States, let alone in underdeveloped economies.

Second is the very definition of "subsistence." In Stanfield's case, this includes the cost of satisfying "prevailing standards of what is necessary for health, efficiency, the nurture of children, and for participation in community activities."[7] In order to reflect the increasing standards of living, the revisions of the budget during the 1960s included payment of mortgage principal, interest payments and insurance costs. This is possibly an adequate budget for a "modest but adequate" level of living in the United States, although it is far from clear to what extent such a budget can be used as a measure of "subsistence". Estimation of the surplus on the basis of this concept as subsistence does not actually measure the surplus. It measures how large the surplus would have been, if all individuals had enjoyed the "modest but adequate" consumption basket. The later discussion in relation to Lippit's definition applies here as well: assuming that some people consume more than they do anticipates the disposition of the surplus.

In sum, the works discussed here have not succeeded in defining "subsistence" in a way that does not contradict the basic idea of a surplus: that it is something that is not necessary for the maintenance of the system and the size and composition of which might have an important impact on the rate and pattern of economic growth.

The Distinction between "Productive" and "Unproductive"

In classical political economy, an unproductive worker is an employed worker who does not contribute to the formation of a surplus. Consequently, it is possible to distinguish between those unproductive workers that do not produce any surplus at all and those that produce a surplus, although smaller than or equal to the subsistence wage; that is, it may sometimes prove useful to distinguish between workers that are unproductive because of the nature of their employment and workers whose productivity is too low to generate a surplus, although the nature of their employment does not prevent surplus generation.

The basic problem in the empirical distinction between productive and unproductive labor is, first, to avoid confusing opinions with analytical results and, second, to achieve consistency between theoretical and operationable concepts. This issue is not solved satisfactorily by Baran. Unproductive labor, according to Baran (1957, 32; emphasis in original), include

> *all labor resulting in the output of goods and services the demand for which is attributable to the specific conditions and relationships of the capitalist system, and which would be absent in a more rationally ordered society.* Thus a good many of these unproductive workers are engaged in manufacturing armaments, luxury articles of all kinds, objects of conspicuous display and marks of social distinction. Others are government officials, members of the military establishment, clergymen, lawyers, tax evasion specialists, public relations experts, and so forth.

It is not quite clear why, for example, public relations experts should be excluded from the productive labor force. It is one thing that one may think of these as undesirable and non-existing in what Baran denotes "a rationally ordered society." It is a completely another thing to claim that public relation experts do not contribute to the formation of a surplus. If "output" means GDP and "surplus" is defined as GDP less essential consumption, public relation experts contribute to the formation of a surplus if private entrepreneurs strive for profit maximization and either (a) their wages exceed subsistence wages and/or (b) the employment of public relations experts increases profits of firms hiring such experts. Public relations experts do not, however, add to the surplus if (a) their wages equal the value of their output *and* (b) their wages are paid out of the existing surplus. In this case, public relations experts would be classified as unproductive labor that produces a surplus no larger than their wage income.[8]

Actual versus Potential Surplus

As was noted, Baran defines a subsistence level per worker and postulates that subsistence consumption (i.e., subsistence per worker times the number of workers) should be deducted from total output in order to arrive at the surplus. Using a similar procedure, Lippit (1985, 11) postulates that the surplus should be calculated by deducting essential consumption *for all members* of society from output.[9] The rationale for this is that "we can regard [essential] consumption as bearing a prior claim on society's output of goods and services." A similar procedure is, as has been seen, followed by Stanfield (1974, 21-27) and in a more recent study by Lippit (1992, 80-85). What do these definitions imply for the interpretation of surplus?

Clearly, this depends on what one is trying to measure. If the objective is to gain a better understanding of development dynamics, which seems to be the case for Baran as well as for Lippit, it is difficult to understand how an arbitrary reallocation of resources can help comprehension. The following example may serve as an illustration. Imagine an economy in which capitalists earn as profits 100 per period, employed workers (10 in number) earn 10 each per period and where there are 10 members of society that do not work. Abstracting from capital depreciation and government activities, national income is 200 per period. Assume that essential consumption has been estimated to 8 per capita per annum. Assuming that capitalists are not allowed any essential consumption, it follows from Lippit's definitions that the total subsistence requirements are 160 (8 for each of the 20 members of society), leaving a surplus of 40.

There are several problems in this approach. First, what is the distribution of the surplus? Each employed worker earns 2 in "excess" wages and capitalists—who are not granted any essential consumption—earn 100. The sum of profits and "excess" wages is 120—far more than the surplus. According to which rule should the surplus of 40 be allocated between workers and capitalists? Even postulating that the entire surplus is in the hands of the capitalists, how should the remaining 60 units of profits be labeled? Since surplus is defined as value of output less subsistence consumption, it follows, from this example, that 60 units of essential consumption are in the hands of the capitalists.

Second, and perhaps more importantly, what are the relations between surplus and development: how can such a definition of surplus facilitate an understanding of economic change? It is difficult to understand why the role of capitalists in the development process should be judged with regard to a surplus income of 40—or, if "excess" wages are defined as surplus, 20—rather than the more intuitively appealing 100 (i.e., the entire profit income).

Third, the "mechanics of the model" remain unclear. If the Baran-Lippit-Stanfield procedure for calculating surplus is accepted, the rights of surplus disposal must also be made clear. Lippit (1985, 1) suggests that surplus may be interpreted as society's "discretionary" income: "At the heart of understanding . . . the surplus is the idea that a great deal may be revealed by examining the manner in which society disposes of what might be thought of as its 'discretionary' income, the income above and beyond what is necessary to meet its socially determined subsistence requirements."

Although of course it is possible to imagine an economy in which "society" allocates its resources after having provided subsistence for all citizens, such an approach for the study of real economies is potentially deceptive. It is a fact that "society" does not meet subsistence requirements; nor does "society" dispose of income. By following Lippit's procedure, the fundamentally antagonistic relations between classes and between individuals and the state are at risk of being ignored. If surplus is to have any meaning for the study of development dynamics in real economies, the definition must recognize the actual distribution of income. Capitalists' behavior is not determined by what they would have left if part of their profit would have been used—by "society"—to fulfill subsistence requirements for all members of society.

AN ALTERNATIVE DEFINITION OF THE SURPLUS

It has been demonstrated that the surplus concepts developed by Baran, Lippit, Riskin and Stanfield can be questioned, albeit on different grounds. It will be argued in what follows that it is possible to derive a definition of surplus from the national accounts that avoids these problems.

To some extent, the desirable qualities of a surplus concept are determined, of course, by the purpose of the study. For anyone who wishes to deal with surplus formation in rural South India, for instance, it is undoubtedly desirable to have a surplus concept that clearly distinguishes between productive and unproductive activities in the informal credit market. For a study which is concerned with surplus formation in the United States, it might be of more value to have a surplus concept that distinguishes between productive and unproductive activities for the suppliers to the armament industry.

It seems, however, to be no exaggeration to claim that the potential value of the empirical surplus approach lies in comparative and long-term studies— investigations that either are concerned with comparing the relations between, on the one hand, the size, distribution and disposition of the surplus and, on the other, the rate and pattern of economic growth in a number of countries or that examine the effects on the rate and pattern of economic growth of changes in the size of the surplus and the like. In particular, such studies would seem to reflect the spirit of Classical Political Economy, both because the relations between surplus and economic growth would be stressed and because long-run development would be emphasized. In addition, such an approach would seem to harmonize with Lippit's (1985, 8) statement that one of the major reasons for studying surplus is to "grasp the dynamics underlying the process of development or underdevelopment in existing economies."

A useful and empirically meaningful surplus concept should therefore, first, be based on data that are regularly published and internationally comparable and, second, its definitions should be consistent with those used in the data set. It is argued here that it is possible to derive a surplus definition with these qualities.[10]

Consider the "income definition" of GDP at purchasers' values:

$$(3.1) \qquad\qquad Y = W + \Pi + \delta K + T_i - Z,$$

where Y is GDP, W is wages, Π is profits, δK is depreciation of capital, T_i is indirect taxes and Z is subsidies. Profits—which in the national accounts are denoted "Operating Surplus"—are gross of taxes and include investment funds and dividends. Assume that "subsistence" is defined as a specified annual wage rate, s, and that the object is to measure the *actual* surplus.[11] Surplus equals output less subsistence. From (3.1) surplus, S, is defined as

$$(3.2) \qquad\qquad S = Y - \delta K - sL = eL + \Pi + T_i - Z,$$

where e is the "excess" wage rate and all employed labor is assmed to be productive.[12] Further denoting productive labor by subscript p and unproductive by subscript u, (3.2) changes to

$$(3.3) \qquad\qquad S = Y - sL_p - \delta K = eL_p + wL_u + \Pi + T_i - Z.$$

Necessary costs of production include depreciation of capital and subsistence wages to productive workers; the remainder is surplus.

As seen, a major problem is to define the level of essential consumption. Most authors have relied on the level of consumption of the working class, estimates of poverty lines and related concepts or levels of sectoral wages. These are all open to criticism, either because the data required may be difficult to come by or because the interpretations seem to raise difficult issues.

It is, however, possible to use the labor income in agriculture as a measure of subsistence. According to the theory of dual economic development, the economy can be divided into two sectors with the use of reproducible capital as the demarcation line.[13] In the traditional sector is thus included not only traditional, small-scale agriculture, but also activities in the "informal" urban sub-sector. The modern sector comprises "the rest of the economy." Economic growth occurs because labor is transferred from the traditional to the modern sector. As long as the wage in the latter sector exceeds the wage in the former, the labor supply facing the modern sector will be "unlimited," which implies that the share of profit in national income increases under growth.

The average wage in agriculture can be interpreted as the subsistence wage because the wage in the traditional sector is the opportunity cost for any modern sector worker: unless the modern sector remuneration exceeds the remuneration in the traditional sector, workers will not be willing to labor in the modern sector.[14] There are two principal reasons why modern sector wages would exceed traditional sector labor remuneration.

First, the cost-of-living in the modern sector may exceed that in the traditional sector. This is likely to occur in particular if the traditional sector is defined as the rural areas and the modern sector as the urban areas (and in this case different price deflators have to be used for the different sectors). Second, the real wage in the modern sector may exceed the real wage in the traditional sector. Again, using the distinction rural/urban rather than traditional/modern, it can be argued that minimum wage legislation often applies to urban areas only; that trade unions are often stronger in urban areas; that large, foreign-owned companies wish to improve their public relations by paying higher wages; that rural workers have some access to non-marketed goods, thus making the average consumption in rural areas higher than what is reflected in incomes in rural areas; or simply that labor markets are imperfect, due, for example, to monopsony power of rural producers.

All in all, this is an argument in favor of using the traditional sector wage as a measure of subsistence. If the real wage in the modern sector exceeds the real wage paid in the traditional sector, this is simply interpreted in terms of modern sector labor receiving a share of the surplus. Traditional sector labor, however, does not receive any part of the surplus: since the agricultural sector is frequently the least productive, agricultural wages are frequently lower than wages in other sectors. The average agricultural wage may therefore be interpreted as the "conventionally determined subsistence level".

As long as interest is focused on the estimation of the surplus for one country for a relatively short period of time, the precise definition of the surplus is of little interest: The finding that surplus constitutes 60 percent of GDP in one particular year has little meaning unless viewed in the proper context. The concept of surplus is related to societal processes, so it is of interest mainly in a dynamic or a comparative context. It is only when the time period under study is so long that it may be suspected that society's conception of "subsistence" changes significantly, that the definition must adjust accordingly. Although it is possible to accommodate this in principle by the use of, say, poverty lines, the data problems are substantial to say the least.

In (3.2) and (3.3), surplus is defined as the net domestic product less subsistence payments to productive workers, that is, subsistence payments to workers producing a surplus. It was noted that the classification of labor as productive and unproductive, respectively, can cause problems. Recall also the discussion in Chapter 2 regarding the classical economists' treatment of this problem and the fact that the distinction is central in their theory of economic growth.

It was noted that unproductive labor can be defined as labor that does not contribute to the formation of a surplus, and that such labor conceptually can be classified as either labor that does not produce any surplus at all and labor that produces a surplus that does not exceed the value of the subsistence wage. Assuming that capitalists attempt to maximize profits, it follows from (3.3) that all labor employed in private firms is productive.[15] A profit-maximizing capitalist will not employ additional workers if this does not contribute to profits. Since profits are part of the surplus, it follows that privately employed labor generates a surplus.[16] It is important to stress that this definition is possible only by defining output in terms of money value. The employment of an additional, previously unemployed worker will increase GDP with at least the value of his wage; employment of additional private labor increases GDP by the wage plus additional profits. Hence, if employment is increased, surplus increases as well. However, if in a state of full employment one firm hires additional labor aggregate surplus does not necessarily increase: it is possible that surplus is simply redistributed between firms (and, plausibly, in favor of labor since the firm probably will have to offer higher wages to attract additional labor). Although the employment of, say, a public relations expert in a firm does not add to the amount of surplus goods, it does add to the amount of financial resources controlled by the firm (provided, of course, that the employment of this expert increases profits).

It follows from this discussion that although all privately employed labor is to be classified as "productive," all government labor is "unproductive." Since government activities are financed out of the surplus, and since the value of output in the government sector can be approximated by the value of wage payments in that sector, it follows that no surplus is produced in the government sector; the value of that sector's output corresponds to an equal reduction of the surplus in the private sector (provided that the government's budget is balanced).

The point here is to understand that surplus is important because it can be used either for consumption or for additions to the economy's capital stock, thus expanding the output potential of the economy. As noted in Chapter 2, classical economists emphasized this point. Ricardo (1951, 150) is quite clear on this issue: "When the annual productions of a country more than replace its annual consumption, it is said to increase its capital; when its annual consumption is not at least replaced by its annual production, it is said to diminish its capital. Capital may therefore be increased by an increased production, or by a diminished unproductive consumption."

Surplus financial resources can be transformed into capital goods or into consumer goods in (international or domestic) markets. "Surplus," as well as "output" and "subsistence" are thus defined in terms of money value. To make this procedure sensible, it must also be assumed that the economy can trade internationally. Specifically, it must be assumed that the surplus financial resources can be transformed into capital goods via international trade.

This general definition of the surplus—more specifics on which are presented later—possesses a number of advantages over competing definitions. First, data are easily available. To calculate the surplus, one needs only national accounts data and labor force data. From this material it is possible to calculate not only the size, but also the functional distribution of the surplus— since Π accrues to capitalists, $(T_i - Z)$ is acquired by the government and $(wL_u + eL_p)$ accrues to labor.[17] It is thus possible to construct time series for the analysis of long-run issues, and to compare the development of the surplus in a number of countries.

Second, the definition of subsistence lends itself—within its limitations—to a sensible economic interpretation. If it is assumed (i) that every worker can find employment in the agricultural sector and (ii) that the average agricultural wage is not higher than the average wage in other sectors, it is quite clear that the average agricultural wage is the opportunity cost for labor outside agriculture—whether employed or not. The reason why labor may prefer to be unemployed to working in the agricultural sector will not be discussed here; these are well known (Todaro 1969; Harris & Todaro 1970). What is important is, first, that only subsistence payments to *employed* labor enter the calculation and, second, that in the aggregate, total subsistence payments equal total income received by subsistence workers; there is no confusion between what is and what ought to be

Third, the definitions of "productive" and "unproductive" labor follow a certain logic. As long as output is defined in terms of money value and as long as capitalists are assumed to be profit maximizers it is necessary to treat all private activities as productive, since "productive" means "surplus-generating" and since profit-maximizing capitalists will take no steps that diminish their profit. Abstracting from market activities, the government is entirely dependent on income from taxes and taxation is simply a redistribution of the surplus. Since the value of output from the government sector is *defined* as the value of wages in that sector, it follows that the government sector does not produce any surplus. Hence, it is unproductive.

Forth and finally, the surplus as defined in this book is the *actual* surplus. This deserves to be stressed, since the principal surplus concept in the literature is Baran's "potential economic surplus" (cf. the essays in Davis 1992). Although the Baran surplus measures what could have been if society had been more "rationally ordered," the surplus in this book measures reality. If the purpose of defining a surplus is to examine propositions generated in classical and modern literature, it is clear that the relevant concept is the one that measures the actual surplus—not the one that would have existed if certain conditions had been fulfilled.

Three versions of the surplus are presented here. Each is suited to aid in the analysis of certain issues and all three will be used in the subsequent analysis. Further, if inter-country comparisons are carried out, it is also of interest to compare the relations between the different versions between different countries.

The first version, Surplus I, measures the surplus before direct taxation has been taken into account and with only subsistence costs of productive labor appearing as necessary costs of production. It is part of (3.3) and is reproduced here for convenience:

$$(3.3) \qquad\qquad S_I = eL_p + wL_u + \Pi + T_i - Z,$$

where e is the excess wage rate, w is the market wage, L is labor, Π is profits and $(T_i - Z)$ is net indirect taxes. Subscripts p and u denote productive and unproductive labor, respectively. Profits, Π, accrues to capitalists, net indirect taxes, $(T_i - Z)$, accrues to the government and the remainder goes to the workers. Since indirect taxes and subsidies are included in this definition of the gross domestic product, S_I is as close as possible to the "original" distribution of the surplus—that is, the one between workers and capitalists—without having knowledge of tax incidence.

The second definition, Surplus II, takes into account the fact that the incomes accruing to labor and capitalists are taxed by the government:

$$(3.4) \qquad\qquad S_{II} = e^D L_p + w^D L_u + \Pi^D + T_d + T_i - Z,$$

where T_d denoted revenue form direct taxation and superscript D denoted disposable surplus. It is clear that S_{II} equals S_I in size, and that the government receives a larger share of the former. A comparison of the development of S_I with the development of S_{II} gives an indication of the extent to which the government uses income taxes to extract surplus.

The third and final version of the surplus, Surplus III, defines what might be denoted "investable surplus." It takes the existing production structure as given, and calculates the surplus, given that all profits, taxes and excess wages are treated as surplus (and, thus, investable):

$$(3.5) \qquad\qquad S_{III} = e^D L + \Pi^D + T_d + T_i - Z,$$

where $L \equiv L_p + L_u$ is the entire employed labor force. Comparing the size of of S_{III} with the size of S_I and S_{II} gives a hint to what extent the government uses its extracted surplus to expand the "unproductive" sector; the distribution of S_{III} in relation to the distribution of, in particular, S_I depicts the pattern of financing of the government sector.

Surplus III may appear questionable as a definition of the surplus, since the subsistence cost of maintaining unproductive (government) labor is included in necessary production costs. "Unproductive labor" would thus not only include civil servants and members of the military establishment, but also members of the secret police for instance. Although the maintenance of such organizations perhaps should be treated as surplus disposal, it is included in subsistence payments precisely because excluding some government activities from necessary cost, while including others would lead to the same trap as Baran's: namely, confusion of what ought to be with what is.[18] One important advantage of treating all government labor as unproductive is that it facilitates the study of the factual size, distribution and disposal of the factual surplus. This is primary; a secondary objective might be to examine how the government *should* allocate its resources in order to attain specific objectives.

THE ANALYTICAL SIGNIFICANCE OF SURPLUS

How can these definitions assist in the analysis of underdevelopment? There are several important issues involved. Some of the more important ones are briefly discussed here.

First of all, if subsistence incomes are entirely consumed, all savings are derived from surplus. In this case, with a constant share of surplus being used for unproductive consumption, the size of the surplus determines the flow of savings and thus the rate of investment. As seen in Chapter 2, this is the basic classical mechanism of economic growth.

Assuming that all savings are generated from surplus income is tantamount to postulating that agricultural wage earners do not save. Is this a reasonable assumption? It should be emphasized that the assumption does not imply that agricultural wages are predestined for consumption or that the nature of their income or occupation prevents agricultural laborers from saving. The important thing is that the statistical relation between the flow of savings and the flow of income is such that subsistence incomes are consumed.[19] Although the classical mechanism of surplus-cum-growth relied ultimately on Malthusian population dynamics (Blaug 1978, 45), the present formulation depends on the postulate that changes in the distribution of income between subsistence and surplus affect savings. Specifically, the behavioral assumption might be that the marginal propensity to save is increasing in income. This would ensure that a change in the distribution of income in favor of surplus recipients—at a constant or growing national income—in favor of surplus increases savings and vice versa.

As long as this assumption can reasonably be expected to be fulfilled, the classical hypothesis that surplus contributes to economic growth via the savings-investment link can be formulated; indeed, a large part of the remainder of this book is dedicated to discussing this hypothesis. A logical extension would of course be to formulate different savings behavior for different groups of surplus recipients.

Second, if conditions in the modern sector change—due, say, to changing terms of trade or revised tax rules—conditions in the traditional sector change as well. Specifically, since conditions in the traditional sector are dependent on conditions in the modern sector, the level of subsistence will be affected by virtually any changes—"exogenous" or government induced—affecting conditions in the modern sector. By using the definitions presented in this chapter, it is possible to trace the effects of virtually any intervention in the economy on production, distribution and extraction of surplus. The mechanics of the development of a dual economy are well known from Lewis (1954) and will not be repeated here. The present approach, however, makes it possible to identify the sources of surplus and how these changes over time.[20]

Third, it is possible to identify conflicts between income groups. Specifically, the "struggle over the surplus" can be conceptualized by estimating the functional and sectoral distribution of surplus and by examining the role of the government in this struggle. Specifically, as has been demonstrated by Markos Mamalakis (1971), the government forms coalitions with different groups in society (e.g., capitalists in the export sector). As demonstrated by Danielson (1989, 137-158) this approach is facilitated by the use of a national accounts-based surplus framework and it broadens the analysis to include social as well as political aspects of the "dynamics of development." Using this approach, it is possible to better comprehend the relations between social and political tension on the one hand and the sectoral and functional distribution of the surplus on the other. In Chapter 7, this issue is discussed further.

CONCLUDING REMARKS

In this chapter two major arguments have been formulated. (i) The surplus definition forwarded by Baran (1957) contains a number of flaws both in terms of consistency and in terms of economic interpretability. These flaws are to some extent inherited by other "surplus researchers," such as Ron Stanfield (1973, 1974), Victor Lippit (1985, 1992) and Carl Riskin (1975). The surplus concepts advocated by these researches are of limited empirical usefulness. (ii) It is possible to derive from the national accounts a definition of the surplus that circumvents those defects by not confusing positive with normative statements. In addition, the relative availability and consistency of national accounts data make it possible to use this surplus concept as an analytical concept in the study of long-run changes.

Two observations appear important. First, the surplus, as defined in this chapter, is applicable only to economies in which the agricultural sector depicts the characteristics mentioned earlier. In particular, that sector should not exhibit a higher average annual wage than any other sector in the economy. Most under-developed countries—and possibly a number of developed countries as well—exhibit this characteristic. It is, of course, possible to adjust these identities in order to consider other sectors in which wages may be lower than in the agricultural sector. It is important, however, that the sector that acts as a "subsistence sector" is also capable of absorbing additional labor. This is important because it is necessary that the wage in the subsistence sector can be interpreted as an opportunity cost for all labor.

Second, it follows from the surplus formulations that the surplus decreases if—ceteris paribus—agricultural wages increase. This may appear unfortunate, since an increase of the agricultural wage would probably signify an increase of agricultural productivity and this, in turn, would suggest that "development" has taken place. It is, however, important to realize that surplus is not a variable that should be maximized. In a sense, the surplus is rather an expression for sectoral productivity discrepancies in the economy.[21] It is therefore important to complement simple calculations of the surplus with an analysis of the sources of surplus (cf. Chapter 5). In fact, the result that the surplus and the level of agricultural wages are inversely related illustrates one of the major conflicts in the economy. Since the size of the surplus depends on the level of wages in the agricultural sector "capitalists have a direct interest in holding down productivity of the subsistence workers" (Lewis 1954, 149). The surplus as defined in this book is therefore not only a concept that can be used for the study of development processes but also a concept that assists in the analysis of clashes in the economy. As long as economic growth and development are regarded as social processes, in other words, phenomena determined not merely by economic mechanics, and as long as conflicts between income classes are considered to be of major importance for an economy's future, it is desirable to have concepts that are amenable to existing data but still cover a broader spectrum than the conventional economics nomenclature. This chapter is an attempt in that direction.

NOTES

1. This chapter is a revised version of "The Concept of Surplus and the Underdeveloped Countries. Critique and Suggestions" (*Review of Radical Political*

Economics, Vol. 22: 214-230, 1990). © *Review of Radical Political Economics*. Reprinted by permission of the Union for Radical Political Economics.

2. The lack of a more appropriate term forces the use of the "surplus approach." This should not be confused with the (essentially theoretical) approach taken be followers of Sraffa and members of the so called "post-Keynesian" school. For examples of this approach—apart from Sraffa (1960)—see Broome (1983), Craven (1979), Goodwin (1970), Harcourt (1972), Lichtenstein (1983) or Roncaglia (1978).

3. First, current investment is not included in the potential economic surplus. Second, the categorization is questionable, since luxury consumption appears twice. Third, the potential economic surplus is larger when it is calculated from the "income side" of the Gross National Product (GNP) than if it is calculated from the "output side". See Lippit (1985, 1992).

4. In particular, Lippit (1985), Riskin (1975) and Stanfield (1973, 1974).

5. See, for instance, Pearson (1957) for a witty and, in parts, relevant critique of subsistence as being physiologically or culturally determined.

6. Although it can be argued that living conditions differ sharply between sectors and therefore that subsistence requirements should be sector-specific, it is later argued that the proper procedure is not to equalize sectoral living conditions but to concentrate on opportunity cost (at least as far as data permit). Of course, if the cost of living differs between sectors, sector-specific price deflators will have to be used.

7. The Department of Labor Statistics, *Workers' Budgets in the U.S*, quoted in Stanfield (1973, 11).

8. The employment of additional staff increases surplus for the entire capitalist class (i.e. not only for the capitalist expanding his labor force because the capitalist either employs previously unemployed labor or lures employed labor to change location of work through higher wages). Wage payments and national income (and thus surplus) increase in both cases.

9. The fact that Baran allocates subsistence requirements to all workers whereas Lippit allocate essential consumption to all members of society is of no importance. The two are related through the average labor force participation rate.

10. This is not to deny the importance of collecting data that challenge conventional approaches. Although research must not be governed by the access to and limitations of existing data, national accounts are so potentially valuable that it would be unwise not to exploit the possibilities of using these for surplus calculations.

11. This should not be confused with Baran's "actual economic surplus," which equals current savings.

12. It follows from (3.1) and (3.2) that $W = wL$ and that $w = s + e$, where w is annual wage per man and L is employed labor.

13. The seminal work, which is the one of interest here, is Lewis (1954). Demarcation lines other than the use of reproducible capital may be more appropriate. Although this is not a major point in the present context (since the use of reproducible capital is not recorded in the national accounts, it is not actually used as a demarcation line in the estimation), the interested reader is directed to Sharif (1986) for a full discussion of the meaning and measurement of "subsistence."

14. Clearly, if labor income differs between sectors, the average wage will exceed the opportunity cost and the size of the surplus will consequently be underestimated.

The distribution of income in the traditional sector is thus an important determinant of the surplus, as defined in (3.3). Admittedly, this is a serious problem, which originates from the use of aggregated data. To some extent, objections can be circumvented by estimating the level of subsistence as the *marginal* wage in the traditional sector. Thus, if an estimate of the surplus in year t is wanted, the marginal subsistence wage may be estimated as

(n3.1)
$$\frac{W_t - W_{t-1}}{L_t - L_{t-1}},$$

where W is total subsistence wages and L denotes employed labor in the traditional sector. This measure reflects changes in the subsistence level and might thus be more appropriate in the case of a differentiated traditional sector.

15. Well-known problems appear here. Thus, for instance, servants are productive if employed in private firms (since capitalists maximize profits, they would not hire anyone who did not help them toward this objective), but unproductive if employed in private homes. Similarly, professors in state universities are unproductive whereas professors in private universities are classified as productive. Solving these problems properly requires immense statistical work. For the typical underdeveloped country, however, servants are likely to constitute the largest unproductive group outside the public sector. It is possible, using the national accounts, to classify their contribution as unproductive.

16. It goes without saying that such a definition is more in line with the Smith-Ricardo tradition than with the Marxian. Compare Roll (1992, 150-151; 241-247).

17. Note, however, that profits from public enterprises will be classified as surplus accruing to capitalists. Many countries following the SNA standard of national accounting practice, however, separate public from private activities so the problem is not necessarily serious.

18. "The standards employed by Baran in 'judging' institutional structures," writes Kanth (1987, 84) apropos of *Monopoly Capital*, "were usually rationalist, as in his discussion of 'essential consumption' or 'wasteful consumption', revealing a personalized, idealist and voluntarist critique of the apparent 'irrationality' of capitalism."

19. That is to say, in estimating the "savings function" $H = a + bY$, where H is per capita savings, Y per capita income and a and b are constants, this assumption requires that $-a/b$ exceeds the subsistence wage. Equally important is that total savings out of any income category should not exceed the volume of surplus accruing to that category of recipients.

20. In Chapter 5 and 6, these matters are discussed in the context of Jamaica.

21. The larger the discrepancy between agricultural labor productivity and the economy-wide labor productivity, the larger the surplus—provided, of course, that the wages paid are to some extent determined by, or at least correlated to, labor productivity.

4

Accumulation and the Agricultural Surplus

The analysis of surplus and its role in the process of economic growth has mostly, as seen in Chapter 2, been carried out in terms of the *general* surplus. Since Adam Smith generalized the Physiocratic model, it has been recognized that several types of industries, apart from agriculture, may be productive in the sense that they may be capable of generating an output in excess of what is needed to keep the industry going at the current level of activity. However, modern (that is, post-war) development economics has focused on the agricultural sector in particular and several attempts have been made to locate the ultimate source of growth in the fact that the agricultural sector, for some reason, starts to produce food in excess of its own immediate needs.

Thus, for instance, Bela Balassa (1981, 4-6) notes that industrial development is impossible without a prior expansion of per capita agricultural production. When per capita food production increases, it becomes possible to support workers outside agriculture, that is, a labor potential, which may be used in the industrial sector while maintaining a necessary level of food production, is created. At the same time, however, incomes increase in the agricultural sector (provided, of course, that the agricultural sector is paid for its export of food), which probably triggers off a demand for non-food products. Hence, an agricultural surplus is a necessary precondition for economic growth, not only because it facilitates the transfer of resources into the budding manufacturing sector but also because it creates a market for manufacturing goods (cf. also the discussion in Chapter 5). Hence, it would be possible to argue, along with Kuznets (1961), Bien (1972), Fei and Ranis (1964), Ishikawa (1967), Morrisson and Thorbecke (1990) and several others that the agricultural surplus occupies a particularly important place in the process of economic growth, because without an agricultural surplus industrialization is simply not possible. The resemblance of this argument to the Physiocratic conclusion only emphasizes John Hicks' (1976, 207) observation that although the natural sciences progress in the sense that old truths (e.g. the Ptolemaic system) are replaced with new—and better—truths (the Copernican system), this is not the case in economics: "we cannot escape in the same way from our own past. We may pretend to escape; but the past crowds in on us all the same."[1]

This chapter digresses somewhat, leaving the general argument and instead concentrating on the role and significance of the agricultural surplus. The discussion begins by examining the recent contribution by Morrisson and Thorbecke (1990), which attempts to measure the agricultural surplus by means of a Social Accounting Matrix. It will be argued that this contribution is largely "measurement without theory" and that it is difficult to see how their method throws any light on the role of surplus (or, for that matter, the agricultural sector) in the process of economic growth. Next is an examination of how surplus is formed in an agricultural sector based on independent small-holders and here it is argued that, in such a system, the problem is not only surplus *formation* but surplus *realization* as well: independent peasants may choose to enjoy increasing productivity as less work rather than more food. This raises the question of appropriate methods of surplus extraction and a final section discusses how the state can extract and possibly transform that surplus into food or other resources necessary for industrialization.

THE MEANING OF THE AGRICULTURAL SURPLUS

A Social Accounting Matrix (SAM) is a convenient tool for organizing data. Although it can be used for virtually any kind of data for which double-entry bookkeeping is appropriate, the following discussion focuses on production and income in sectors. This means that an outflow of commodities is balanced by an inflow of money and vice versa. The SAM contains most of the information found in the national accounts, but, in addition, it can provide information on the distribution of income among different household groups.[2] The SAM is divided into several accounts, each occupying one row and one column. If columns are denoted "Expenditures" and rows "Receipts," the column n shows how the expenditures of the socioeconomic group n are divided between different activities and similarly for row n. In principle, then, the SAM works just like any input-output table with the important proviso that although an input-output table tells something about the interdependence between production sectors in an economy, the SAM provides information on the flow of goods and payments between different socioeconomic groups.

Christian Morrisson and Erik Thorbecke (1990) utilize a SAM to define and calculate the agricultural surplus. They define six different accounts—factors of production, institutions, production activities, government, the capital account and the rest of the world—and within each account they distinguish between agricultural and non-agricultural activities. The surplus is defined by Morrisson and Thorbecke (1990, 1081, emphasis in original) as "a flow of resources from agriculture to nonagriculture which is *not compensated*." Thus if agricultural households pay $100 million in taxes and receive $75 million in investments and subsidies, the non-compensated outflow from the agricultural household sector to the government is $25 million. By summing the net flows of resources from agricultural households to the rest of the economy, Morrisson and Thorbecke are able to calculate the agricultural surplus generated in agricultural households; and by repeating this procedure for the agricultural activities in the remaining accounts the total agricultural surplus is defined as the sum of these net flows.

Several features should be noted. First, it is, in principle, possible to calculate the surplus for any account or for non-agricultural activities as well. Also, if the rest of the world is taken into account, it can be noted that the global surplus is equal to zero (a positive surplus in one activity corresponds to a negative surplus in other activities; this follows from the properties of double entry bookkeeping). The existence of a surplus in the Morrisson and Thorbecke approach, then, is simply a reflection of some activities receiving less resources than paid for. A surplus in the government sector, for instance, means that the government receives less income in taxes and interest than it spends on consumption, transfers and investments. Such a surplus would thus be equivalent to a public sector deficit.

Second, it is difficult to understand the rationale of defining surplus in this way. As discussed at length in Chapter 2, a surplus is generally defined as resources in excess of what is necessary to maintain the current level of activity. If an economy produces 400 tonnes of food this year and if this process uses 1,000 manhours, 100 acres of land, 10 tonnes of fertilizers and $1 million to repair machines, any income emanating from the sale of this food that is in excess of what is necessary to buy these inputs is a surplus. For Morrisson and Thorbecke, an agricultural surplus is something that flows from agriculture to another sector without the agricultural sector being appropriately compensated for this. Hence, the fact that the agricultural sector pays taxes in excess of what it receives in return from the government in the example just provided is evidence of a positive agricultural surplus. Using the conventional definition that surplus is production in excess of what is needed to maintain the existing level of production, it follows from Morrisson and Thorbecke's approach that *the entire agricultural surplus is always appropriated by other activities*. In other words, the level of income in the agricultural sector is always precisely sufficient for maintaining the current level of production.

Third, as is recalled from Chapter 2, the surplus in classical analysis is always non-negative. This is the viability condition, which follows from the very definition of "subsistence." If total output falls short of total subsistence, the level of activity falls until the viability condition is met. In the Morrisson and Thorbecke approach, however, a negative agricultural surplus is perfectly possible. This would simply mean that agricultural activities receive from other activities more than what flows out. If the agricultural sector does not pay taxes, but receives production subsidies from the government, the net flow of resources out of agriculture is negative and so is the agricultural surplus. In fact, Morrisson and Thorbecke (1990, 1086-1088) provide a numerical illustration of Indonesia with the result that the 1980 agricultural surplus amounted to approximately —329 billion rupiahs, some 0.7 percent of GNP. This means that the agricultural sector received goods and services worth 329 billion rupiahs in excess of what was produced in that sector in that year. If a positive surplus is positively related to economic growth, a negative surplus could reasonably be expected to retard growth. It is difficult to understand why imports of high-yielding rice varieties and large-scale use of fertilizers (the explanation for the negative surplus suggested by Morrisson and Thorbecke) would impede economic growth.

In conclusion, the method for measuring the agricultural surplus suggested by Morrisson and Thorbecke does not seem to aid an understanding of the relations between economic expansion and surplus formation. Quite the contrary, the SAM approach to the agricultural surplus seems to be measurement without theory and, as such, it is difficult to understand patterns of growth and stagnation from a surplus point of view by using a SAM (although the SAM, of course, may be quite useful for other purposes, such as planning or simulation exercises). As long as one sticks to the classical approach, it would seem more appropriate to distinguish between social classes, since it might be presumed that these show different behavior, in particular regarding surplus disposal.

However, it is also important to understand that the surplus approach presented in Chapter 3 is not applicable to all situations. In some economies, it is simply not the relevant instrument. Recall that subsistence is defined as the average agricultural wage, agricultural laborers being the only group that cannot receive surplus. As long as it is possible to distinguish between different types of income, the surplus method may be used, but when consideration turns to the "pure peasant economy" (to be defined shortly) the surplus defined as the difference between value of output and the average agricultural wage ceases to have any meaning. Since the pure peasant economy consists only of independent farmers, tilling their land with the aid of their own labor, "wage" and "income" become synonymous.[3] In such an economy, then, the average agricultural wage would be equivalent to the average agricultural income and total wages equal to total income so a surplus, in the sense of Chapter 3, could not exist. To see how and why a "surplus" may arise in a pure peasant economy, then, such an economy should be studied in detail. This will prove to be an instructive detour, since it will reveal that producers in the pure peasant economy may choose not only the *size* of their surplus but the *composition* as well.

SURPLUS IN THE PURE PEASANT ECONOMY

The pure peasant economy is defined as an economy in which independent farmers till the land with the aid of their own labor. Whether capital is used in the production process depends on whether the peasants have access to capital goods—either by devoting time to making these or by exchanging food for capital goods. Looking first at how decisions are made in an economy in which there is no capital reveals how the peasants' decisions are affected by external factors (e.g., population growth or changing terms of trade with the outside world). Although the discussion is framed within the standard model of the peasant household as exposed, for example, by Nakajima (1969) and Sen (1966), it is postulated that peasants are capable of changing the technique of production at their will along the lines suggested by Boserup (1965).

The Basic Model

In Boserup (1965), a number of "stylized facts" are important. As will be noted, however, these more or less follow from any well-behaved neoclassical production function. First, output per labor hour falls as the labor:land ratio increases (i.e., as the production technique changes): "when shortening of fallow leads to the clearing of bush instead of secondary forest and hoeing and weeding becomes necessary ... yields per hectare are likely to decline considerably. Hence there is a strong presumption that the transition ... will be accompanied by a decline in output per man-hour" (Boserup, 1965, p. 30), and "to shorten the period of fallow, output per man-hour is likely to decline considerably for all cultivators" (Boserup, 1965, p. 33).

Second, it is explicitly stated that an increasing labor:land ratio (intensification) is accompanied by an increase in the length of the average working day: "we may view the changes in agricultural employment brought about by population growth and intensification of land use ... as a gradual lengthening of work hours in agriculture" (Boserup, 1965, p. 53).

Hence, the distinction between "laborers" and "labor hours" is vital, since there is not necessarily any unique relation between the labor force participation rate (measured as the share of household members in the labor force) and labor input (measured as the number of family hours worked).

The family—consisting of m members—produce a homogenous output using homogenous labor and land according to

(4.1) $$Y = Y(T,H); \quad Y_T, Y_H \geq 0; Y_{TT}, Y_{HH} \leq 0,$$

where Y is output, T is acres of land, H is hours of labor and subscripts denote partial derivatives. The amount of land available is fixed. Cultivation techniques are *defined* as the land-labor ratio, Φ. Furthermore, two limiting techniques exist. One, Φ_1, for which $\partial Y/\partial T = 0$ and one, Φ_2, for which $\partial Y/\partial H = 0$, with $\Phi_1 > \Phi_2$. Between these a continuum of techniques exists, all of which are known to the family.[4] The family maximizes utility according to

(4.2) $$U = U(Y,H); \quad U_Y \geq 0; U_H \leq 0, U_{YY}, U_{HH} \leq 0,$$

where U is an index of family utility.[5] The time available to the family is, of course, fixed and equal to M. It is divided between work, H, and leisure, L.

It is possible to identify the family's minimum consumption requirement, C_{min}. In addition, if the number of family members is m, each family member's minimum consumption requirement is C_{min}/m (for now, it is assumed that all output is consumed). Further, it is possible to identify the maximum amount of labor hours that the family can provide, H_{max}. Denoting the number of working family members as n ($\leq m$), the maximum number of labor hours each member can provide per period is H_{max}/n.

The model is recursive in the sense that the family chooses labor input, H, to maximize the utility function $U[Y(T,H);H]$ subject to the time constraint $M = H + L$. This, in turn, determines technique (since the amount of land available is fixed) and level of output. This yields the familiar equilibrium condition

(4.3) $$-U_H/U_Y = Y_H.$$

The (negative of) the marginal rate of substitution between work and output equals the marginal productivity of labor. Of course, this is a viable solution if and only if the equilibrium pair $(H^*;Y^*)$ is such that $H^* \leq H_{max}$ and $Y^* \geq C_{min}$. If the equilibrium labor input, H^*, is smaller than T^*/Φ_1, where T^* is the area of land available to the family, the most land intensive technique will be employed. If H^* exceeds T^*/Φ_1 a more labor intensive technique will be adopted, with the limiting case being technique Φ_2, at which the marginal productivity of labor equals zero.

How does the family respond to growth of population? As shall be subsequently seen, it depends on *how* the population grows—on how participation in the labor force is affected. Following Nakajima (1969) and Levi (1976/77), the labor force participation rate is defined as $\eta = n/m$ (≤ 1) and it is assumed that the family's marginal valuation of leisure in relation to the marginal valuation of output depends on the labor force participation rate. In particular, when the labor force participation rate falls, due, perhaps, to a decreased infant mortality rate, the marginal valuation of output increases in relation to the marginal valuation of leisure for a given level of labor input . Formally, the marginal rate of subsitution between leisure and output (MRS_{YL}) depends, for every level of labor input, on the labor force participation rate, η:

(4.4) $$MRS_{YL}|_{H=H^*} = \phi(\eta), \; \phi' > 0,$$

where, of course, $MRS_{YL} \equiv U_L/U_Y$ (note that $-U_H \equiv U_L$).

Now, given (4.4), it is easily seen why it is important to distinguish between the case when population growth causes the labor force participation rate to change and the case when it does not. In the case when infant mortality suddenly drops, or working members of the family migrate, the labor force participation rate falls and the family adjusts its equilibrium labor input accordingly.

As long as land is abundant, the family uses technique Φ_1. Here, an expansion of employment is accompanied by a proportionate increase in the amount of land cultivated. Hence, output increases proportionately to employment and the family is consequently employing a technique characterized by the marginal productivity of land being zero. The family's utility is maximized when (4.3) is satisfied—where the marginal rate of substitution between leisure and output equals the marginal productivity of labor. This is the implicit price of family labor, which may differ between families. If this is the case, the emergence of intra-rural labor markets will ensure the equalization of wages. The family's minimum consumption requirement and the number of labor hours available are determined by the number of family members, m, and the number of working members, n. In what follows, it is assumed that the family does not discriminate between male and female labor, so the labor force participation rate will also be stable over time.

Assume now that the size of the family increases from m to m'. Specifically, assume that the rate of infant mortality declines, so that a larger number of children survive, causing a disequilibrium in the family size and composition to which output, labor input and production technique have to be adjusted. First, the family's minimum consumption increases because the number of family members has increased. Since it is assumed that infant mortality declines, the maximum labor available does not change (at least not in the short run). Hence the labor force participation rate has fallen from n/m to n/m'.

The increase of the family size changes the equilibrium MRS as depicted in (4.4). From (4.3) it is clear that a fall in the MRS between leisure and output leads to an adjustment process in which labor input will increase. Hence, population growth implies that the implicit price of family labor falls with consequent effects on intra-rural labor markets. Finally, the technique employed by the family may change as the population grows. If the family initially utilizes all available land, the only way in which output can be increased is by adding more labor to existing land. Hence, the land:labor ratio declines. Note also that while the number of working family members remains constant, labor input increases, so the length of the average working day increases due to agricultural intensification. While total output increases, output per labor hour declines. This is in accord with the stylized facts discussed above. This analysis can be summarized as follows.

If non-working members are added to the family, per capita consumption will—ceteris paribus—fall. The family adjusts to its increasing size by lowering its price of family labor: additional output becomes more valuable in relation to additional leisure so more labor will be employed. Whether this implies that the land:labor ratio declines depends, of course, on whether land is scarce or not. If land is abundant, the area under cultivation is simply expanded, and the family continues to employ the Φ_1 technique. If land is scarce, the family is forced to add more labor to the existing area of land. The land:labor ratio declines and the technique employed changes to a more labor intensive one. The process of adjustment may continue in response to population growth until the technique adopted is characterized by a marginal labor productivity of zero.

The Size and Composition of the Surplus

The intensification process, triggered off by population growth, will eventually come to an end. When the family has adopted the technique characterized by a zero marginal productivity of labor (Φ_2), output cannot—unless the land area is expanded—grow. The economy is still viable, however, since there is room for continuing population growth until the total minimum consumption requirements equal total output. In other words, when the most labor intensive technique is adopted, further growth of population is supported out of the surplus.[6]

However, if the family would be able to improve the productivity (i.e., the quality) of land and/or labor, it would be possible to postpone stagnation. Two principal means for doing so are available: first, by directly using the "surplus" resources generated in the family; second, by trading "surplus" resources for imports. These alternatives will be examined in turn.

The choice of labor input is limited by two constraints: minimum consumption requirements C_{min} and maximum labor supply, H_{max}. Total surplus, S_T, in terms of output, then, is

(4.5) $$S_T = Y(T^*, H_{max}) - C_{min}.$$

Part of the surplus is realized as output; part is enjoyed as leisure. Denoting the food and labor surpluses by indices F and H, respectively, yields

(4.6) $$S_F = Y(T^*, H^*) - C_{min}$$

(4.7) $$S_H = Y(T^*, H_{max}) - Y(T^*, H^*),$$

where T^* and H^* denote equilibrium input of land and labor, respectively, and the labor surplus is expressed in terms of output. By virtue of (4.4), the *composition* of S_T depends entirely on the labor force participation rate. Defining $c_{min} = C_{min}/m$, if land is scarce and if non-working members are added to the household, total surplus changes by $-c_{min}$. Food surplus changes by $Y_H \phi' - c_{min}$ and labor surplus changes by $-Y_H \phi'$. By (4.4), ϕ' (> 0) denotes the change in the equilibrium labor input that follows a change in the labor force participation rate and Y_H is the marginal product of labor. Hence, the composition of the surplus changes in favor of food as the economy grows and as long as the additional output produced by additional labor exceeds the additional minimum consumption requirements, the food surplus increases in absolute terms.

If the economy is isolated from other sectors (so that inter-sectoral trade is not possible and capital goods are not available), and if the switch to a new technique requires investments, this can be carried out in three ways. First, the family can employ part of the actual labor surplus for investments which thus leaves current output unaffected. Second, part of the potential labor surplus can be allocated to investment tasks. In this case, current output will fall in proportion to labor withdrawn. Finally, labor can be hired to do investment tasks. In this case, hired labor is paid with food, which leaves less output for family consumption. The actual choice between these alternatives depends on a number of factors. Clearly, if per capita consumption is not allowed to decline, it is likely that investments are taken care of by allocating parts of the actual labor surplus to these tasks. When population grows, the labor force participation rate falls so the composition of S_T changes in favor of S_F. The implication of this is that the scope for labor intensive investment in the closed economy diminishes as population grows. Since labor intensive preparations in the form of irrigation or terracing are most likely to be important in the later stages of intensification, it is conceivable (although not intuitively obvious) that the intensification process may be temporarily halted because of labor shortage. However, the food surplus, as share of total surplus, increases as the population grows so the scope for intersectoral trade, exchanging food for other goods, increases.

Now, assume that the family is given the opportunity of trading with other sectors in the economy. Specifically, assume that the family can import manufactured consumption goods. The marginal utility of output increases to the family (since it now has a wider variety of commodities to purchase), so, for every level of labor input, the marginal valuation of output in relation to the marginal valuation of leisure increases. Consequently, the effects on labor utilization, production level and surplus composition are virtually the same when intersectoral trade is allowed as when the non-working population grows. One important implication is that the farming family can be stimulated to increase output if it is offered attractive manufactured goods in exchange.

Compared to the SAM-analysis by Morrisson and Thorbecke (1990), the present approach seems to better capture the actual workings of a pure peasant economy. Several important conclusions appear. First, the agricultural surplus consists of a mix of food and leisure and changes in this mix are essentially determined by the family's response to population growth. This means that if the government seeks to extract surplus, it has to apply different methods depending on whether the total agricultural surplus consists predominantly of food or of leisure. In the latter case, the more efficient method of surplus extraction might be to create attractive opportunities for work outside the peasant economy, whereas in the former case taxes might serve the government's purposes. Irrespective of the composition of the surplus, however, peasants in an economy that is not isolated make their choices regarding the volume and technique of production on the basis of how much investment goods or manufactured goods they will receive in return for export of a given volume of food. Hence, the terms of trade between sectors are an important determinant of the distribution of the surplus. As shall be seen in the next section, manipulation of the terms of trade has often been an attractive tool for transferring the agricultural surplus to other sectors of the economy.

ALTERATION OF RELATIVE PRICES

The issue of terms of trade manipulations in favor of the industrial sector duplicates to some extent the Great Industrialization Debate in the Soviet Union in the 1920s. In particular, it was argued by Evgeny Preobrazhensky that the rate of industrialization could be increased if part of the agricultural surplus was transferred to the industrial sector. Such a policy—Primitive Socialist Accumulation—would be characterized by artificially lowering the price of food relative to the price of manufactured goods. By so doing, profits in the manufacturing sector would increase, so that the scope for industrial accumulation would increase.[7] The essence of "the price scissors model" has been formalized in the work by Raaj Kumar Sah and Joseph Stiglitz (1984).[8]

Sah and Stiglitz construct a "socialist" model of a two-sector economy in which improvements of the industrial sector's terms of trade increase the surplus in that sector and hence the potential for industrial accumulation. The strategic assumption of the model is that the government directly controls the wage of the urban workers (this, presumably, is one of the features rendering the model "socialist"). The size of the marketed surplus of food depends on the domestic terms of trade. Industrial workers spend all their income on food. The surplus is defined as the excess of industrial production over industrial wages and accrues to the government. The number of hours worked in industry is fixed and determined by the government; the supply of labor to the industrial sector, that is to say, is completely inelastic with respect to wages.

Given these assumptions, it is not very difficult to show that a deterioration of the food sector's terms of trade can increase the government's surplus, while maintaining equilibrium in the food market. First, given employment and technology in the industrial sector, the size of the surplus is determined by the industrial wage rate in relation to labor productivity (which, it is recalled, is set by the state). Decreasing that rate, ceteris paribus, increases the state's surplus. Second, the marketed surplus of food is determined by the domestic terms of trade: lowering the relative price of food lowers the amount of food marketed. It follows that, for every level of domestic terms of trade, there exists an industrial wage rate for which the food market is equilibrium. It also follows that a deterioration of the food sector's terms of trade must, in order to ensure continuing equilibrium in the food market, be accompanied by a lower industrial wage rate.[9] Since the number of hours worked in industry is fixed by the state, a decrease of the industrial wage rate does not affect industrial output. Hence, the state's surplus (defined as industrial output in excess of industrial wages) is increased as the relative price of food is lowered.[10]

Given the assumptions made, the conclusion reached by Sah and Stiglitz is not very path breaking. What they illustrate is the relatively trivial thesis that an inelastic supply is not responsive to changes in prices: their results critically hinge on the assumption that the industrial labor supply is completely inelastic, or—which amounts to the same thing—that the state is perfectly capable of determining urban real wages. To generalize, assume now that the economy is dual and not "socialist." The food producing sector consists of small-holders exhibiting a positive price elasticity for marketed supply. The industrial sector consists of workers and capitalists. The industrial sector faces an unlimited supply of labor at a wage fixed in terms of food.

If the food market is initially in equilibrium, a deterioration of the food sector's terms of trade lowers the amount of food supplied. To restore food market equilibrium industrial workers' demand for food must fall. The extent to which the real industrial wages should be cut to restore food market equilibrium depends, of course, on the relation between food producers' output elasticity and industrial workers' income elasticity for food. As long as the latter exceeds the former, deterioration of the food sector's terms of trade increases the state's scope for surplus extraction, for example, through taxation of industrial wages.

This and other conclusions can be illustrated using some simple notation.[11] Assume that the supply of marketed surplus is determined by the domestic terms of trade, p, and that the demand for food is determined by labor income, W, and the domestic terms of trade:

(4.8) $m = m(p)$

(4.9) $f = f(W, p).$

Let ε_m and ε_f denote output elasticity of marketed supply and income elasticity with respect to food, respectively:

(4.10) $\varepsilon_m = (dm/dp)(p/m)$

(4.11) $\varepsilon_f = (\partial f/\partial W)(W/f).$

An alteration of domestic terms of trade (Δp) changes marketed output of food by $\varepsilon_m(\Delta p/p)$. To maintain balance in the food market, the demand for food must change by an equal amount, that is, $\varepsilon_f(\Delta W/W) = \varepsilon_m(\Delta p/p)$, or the change of wages must satisfy

(4.12) $\Delta W = (\varepsilon_m/\varepsilon_f)\Delta p(W/p).$

The industrial wage rate is $w = vp$, where $p = p_a/p_m$ is the domestic terms of trade in terms of manufactured goods and v is the (fixed) wage rate in terms of food. It follows that a deterioration of the food sector's terms of trade increases the real industrial wage. To maintain $w/p=v$, part of the industrial wage must be extracted. On the other hand, the deterioration of the relative price of food increases industrial demand for food. To restore balance in the food market, the industrial demand for food must be cut, first, to counteract the increasing demand following from the alteration of relative prices and, second, to diminish the purchasing power of industrial workers since the marketed supply of food has diminished. This can be attained by imposing taxes on food marketed in the industrial sector. The relative sizes of the taxes on industrial wage income and on food depend, respectively, on the price elasticity for food in the industrial sector and the output elasticity of marketed supply in the food producing sector.

Changing the domestic terms of trade thus alters the sectoral composition of income and hence of the surplus. By reducing the price of agricultural goods relative to manufacturing goods, a share of the surplus is transferred to the manufacturing sector. Since this policy increases the purchasing power of wages in the industrial sector, the taxable capacity of that sector increases.

Alteration of domestic terms of trade is thus a method with which the state can transfer part of the surplus from sectors in which the cost of taxation is high to sectors from which incomes can be taxed to a lower cost. Although the government clearly can manipulate the domestic terms of trade in order to redistribute surplus, it is a generally held view that agriculture carries indirectly a significant tax burden. According to the seminal paper by Wyn Owen (1966), agriculture in underdeveloped countries—whether socialist or not—is exposed to a "double developmental squeeze." Although the political color of the regime determines the exact manner in which these squeezes are applied, they are nevertheless similar for both capitalist and socialist economies.

The double developmental squeeze has two aspects: the production squeeze and the expenditure squeeze. The production squeeze, in what Owen denotes "the Marxist-Leninist approach," takes the form of compulsory deliveries of farm products at artificially low prices, as in Stalin's Soviet Union (although collectivization does not necessarily follow), or a combination of high farm prices and high farm taxes, as in Meiji Japan. The approach used in Japan during the turn of the century consisted of, first, artificially high prices to farmers in order to stimulate production and make land investments pay and, second, high farm taxes (mostly taxes on land) in order to extract agricultural profits. By using this variant of the production squeeze, the Japanese government ensured that the urban food demand could be domestically satisfied (Ranis 1959). The argument advanced here that the government turns the domestic terms of trade against agriculture is based on the assumption that extraction costs are smaller in non-agriculture than in agriculture. This was probably not the case in Meiji Japan. The efficient administration, the extended systems of controls and the relatively concentrated pattern of landownership were all factors encouraging the government to stimulate agriculture. To replicate the Meiji pattern of surplus extraction, however, it is necessary to replicate the low costs of surplus extraction in agriculture.

It could be questioned to what extent Owen is correct in putting Stalin's Soviet Union and Japan after the Meiji restoration under the same (Marxist-Leninist) hat. What they have in common is not ideology, but the extent to which the government takes active part in the extraction process. Owen shows, however, that the production squeeze can occur even if there is no government ready to interfere with the market. This—which Owen calls the "Mill-Marshallian model"—simply takes the form of competition (Owen claims to have found empirical evidence for its existence by studying the economic development of the United States).

In order to reap profits and to keep pace with his competitors, the individual farmer in the Mill-Marshallian setup must continuously invest in new techniques. This increases the supply of farm products to the non-agricultural sector at successively lower prices: "Competition giveth (by fostering technological progress) and competition taketh away (by taking excess profits)" (Yotopoulos & Nugent 1976, 261).

In the Mill-Marshallian model, therefore, the agricultural sector faces deteriorating terms of trade, which, together with the rapidly progressing technology, leads to a relative decline of agriculture's size. Only the most efficient farmers are able to profit from the declining prices of farm products, and a decreasing number of increasingly productive farmers are able to support the entire non-agricultural population with farm products. The rest of the farm population has to seek their living elsewhere. Specifically, Owen recognizes the possibility of rural-urban migration for farmers left behind in the technological race. This flow of labor and human capital from the agricultural sector constitutes the second aspect of the double developmental squeeze: labor raised and educated in the agricultural sector flow to non-agriculture. Since agriculture may function as a well in which labor is maintained until it can be absorbed in non-agriculture, rural-urban migration can imply substantial migration of (human) capital as well.

It is clear that the double developmental squeeze can be encouraged by the government—"Marxist-Leninist" or "Mill-Marshallian". For example, by subsidising capital investment in agriculture in order to reduce the demand for labor in that sector, or by taxing agricultural land, the government expedites the structural transformation of the economy. In addition, if the non-agricultural sector is favored—for example, by low taxes, subsidies or protection—its expansion is likely to be relatively rapid, which amplifies the squeeze on resources.

CONCLUDING REMARKS

The agricultural surplus occupies a special place in the history of economic analysis. From the Physiocratic emphasis of the sterility of all non-agricultural activities to modern development theory, a viable (and possibly growing) agricultural sector is a prerequisite for successful economic growth. Sometimes, however, it seems as if the emphasis of agriculture overshadows other important aspects of the development process. Although it is true that the agricultural surplus may be strategic in certain phases of development, it is important to realize that as soon as a viable manufacturing sector has come into existence, an economy that is open to international trade may purchase its necessary food from abroad rather than from a domestic agriculture.

Such a strategy, however, is not among those generally chosen by developing countries. Since the cost of labor in the manufacturing sector can be fixed in terms of food, rulers seem to have often been attracted by the prospect of simply keeping food prices artificially low in order to increase the surplus in the manufacturing sector and thereby speed up industrialization. As seen in this chapter, however, the agricultural surplus in the pure peasant economy is not easy for rulers to extract and control for farmers may respond to attempts at extraction by simply turning food into leisure and thereby rendering it even more difficult for rulers to get a piece of the pie.

The chapters that follow takes a close look at one economy in which fiscal policies illustrate very well the points made here. Analyzing Jamaica under the leadership of Michael Manley (1972-80) reveals that Manley's attempts of turning the distribution of the surplus in favor of certain groups severely damaged the prospects for economic growth in Jamaica—an economy whose performance in the 1960s was often described in terms of "success" and "miracle."

NOTES

1. See Lewis (1988) for evidence that this is true especially for development economics and Mankiw (1990, 1646-1647) for a similar argument regarding modern macroeconomics.

2. A more detailed description of the workings of a SAM is provided in the collection edited by Pyatt and Round (1985) and in particular by King (1985). Note also that the *Tableau Économique,* as discussed in Chapter 2 may be interpreted as a SAM, since it focuses on the links between the structure of production and the distribution of income (Stone, 1985, Appendix).

3. This is so unless one works with imputed wages—something that demands that the opportunity cost can be defined. In a pure peasant economy, this is, as shall be seen, a purely subjective concept.

4. That is, it is assumed that the existing techniques are sufficient in number to make the composite function imitate a well-behaved production function. The continuity assumption is made for expositional convenience. As has been demonstrated by, for example, Findlay (1973, Ch. 6), if it is assumed instead that isoquants are discontinuous between Φ_1 and Φ_2, the major results of the analysis are not affected. Basically, not assuming continuity results in the possibility that the family will use two production techniques simultaneously arises. This, however, adds nothing substantial to the analysis.

5. The well-known problems regarding inter-personal comparisons of utility are ignored. There are two principal ways of avoiding this problem. First, it can be assumed that all members of a given household have identical tastes and utility functions. Second, it might be assumed that one person in the household—the household dictator—takes all decisions. It is also possible to ignore the problem completely by following Sen (1966, 426) who assumes that "peasants have not heard of difficulties of interpersonal comparisons of utility and make such comparisons blatantly."

6. Strictly speaking the situation can be interpreted as one in which additional population is supported out of the surplus *before* technique Φ_2 has been employed since—as shown later—the volume of surplus is likely to fall as a consequence of population growth. When technique Φ_2 is adopted, however, and the population continues to grow, the entire consumption of the additional population comes from the surplus.

7. Compare Preobrazhensky (1965), in particular Chapter 2 and Appendix, and Erlich (1950).

8. See also comments by Blomqvist (1986) and Carter (1986), and the reply by Sah and Stiglitz (1986).

9. This presupposes, of course, that food in the urban market is a normal good.

10. According to Sah and Stiglitz (1984), the conclusion that the state can increase the investable surplus by altering the domestic terms of trade is one of Preobrazhensky's two propositions, the other being that this accumulation is possible without deteriorating the living standard of the industrial workers (welfare in the food producing sector, of course, declines).

11. More detailed analyses of the effects of alteration of the domestic terms of trade can be found in, inter alia, Dixit (1969). Zarembka (1970), Reynolds (1969) and Hornby (1968). Compare, however, the view put forward by Lipton (1977, 288): "Nor need we decide if the terms of trade have 'moved against' agriculture—that is, whether a unit of farm sales commands more or less farm and farm-household purchases than previously. This is an arbitrary exercise, because its outcome depends on what 'previously' is." Lipton's view is challenged by Moore (1984).

III

An Application: Jamaica under Manley

5

Size and Distribution of the Surplus

In this and two subsequent chapters an attempt will be made to analyze the economic performance of Jamaica from the points of view developed in Part II. Focus is on the 1970s, in particular because these years represent a period of unusual deep recession in Jamaica's economic history. In addition, between 1972 and 1980, Jamaica was governed by the People's National Party (PNP), headed by Michael Manley, and in what follows it will be argued that the policy of Democratic Socialism pursued by the PNP to some extent was responsible for the economy's dismal performance.[1]

However, before plunging into calculations of the size and distribution of the surplus it is important to outline some of the basic features of "normal" economic development: what is the long-run pattern of growth and structural change in successful developing countries?

ECONOMIC DEVELOPMENT: SOME STYLIZED FACTS

Following the studies of Chenery (1979) and his associates, the structural changes in the "normal," industrializing economy accompanying a secular increase of per capita incomes are roughly as follows (Kirkpatrick & Nixon 1984, 17-19).

- The share of agriculture in GDP declines and the share of manufacturing industry increases.
- The share of the total labor force in the manufacturing sector increases, while the share of the labor force in agriculture declines.
- The composition of manufacturing output changes in favor of heavy industry, such as electricity, chemicals and transport equipment.

- The share of heavy industry employment increases more rapidly than light industry employment although the latter accounts for a larger part of absolute growth in manufacturing employment.

The process is initiated by an increase in agricultural incomes. This generates a domestic demand for non-agricultural products and "more often than not, it is associated with export expansion" (Balassa 1981, 4). The opportunity to exchange food for non-agricultural commodities provides peasants with an incentive to increase food production in excess of their own consumption. This leads to an increase in the volume of exports and inter-sectoral trade. The non-agricultural sector is able to produce at relatively low costs due to the existence of surplus labor in the food producing sector. The foreign exchange generated by agricultural exports enables the manufacturing sector to import capital goods and raw material, which cannot be produced domestically. Eventually, the domestic manufacturing sector becomes self-supporting with respect to investable capital, since the supply of cheap labor from the agricultural sector ensures the generation of adequate profits.

As the non-agricultural sector grows, the composition of its output changes. In particular, Engel's Law ensures that the pattern of demand for non-agricultural goods in the food producing sector changes as the incomes in that sector increase. As the relative size of the manufacturing sector increases, its trade advantages relative to other countries change in favor of less labor-intensive commodities. Eventually, this stimulates the establishment of a domestic capital goods industry and the gradual substitution of domestically produced raw materials for imported ones. In addition, there is an increase in the degree of vertical integration in the non-agricultural sector due to the growth in the domestic supply of investable capital, entrepreneurship and skilled labor, brought about by the expansion of the manufacturing sector.

There are two fundamental problems that must be solved to ensure the smooth operation of the mechanisms driving this process. First, the supply of food to the manufacturing sector must be sufficient to support a growing industrial labor force. Specifically, the rate of growth of marketed food supply must not be lower than the rate of growth of employment in the manufacturing sector. If the supply of food falls short of demand, the expansion of the manufacturing sector may be arrested, since structural inflation may occur, or the additional food has to be imported, leaving less room for imports of raw materials, capital goods and spare parts. The "food problem" has been solved in various ways in various countries: in Japan, after the Meiji Restoration, favorable prices for food products were combined with high taxes on farm land in order to encourage the efficient use of land by land owners while the tax revenue could be used to subsidize food for the growing manufacturing sector; in Stalin's Soviet Union, food deliveries were made compulsory; and so on. The market solution to the food problem is reflected in the secular deterioration of the food sector's terms-of-trade observed, for example, in the United States: rapid technical progress in the food producing sector ensured the availability of cheap food in the manufacturing sector at the same time as resources were released from the food-producing sector for employment in the manufacturing sector.[2]

The second problem is the generation of sufficient investable funds for the manufacturing sector. According to Simon Kuznets (1961, 70), "one of the crucial problems of modern economic growth is how to extract from the product of agriculture a surplus for the financing of capital formation necessary for economic growth without at the same time blighting the growth of agriculture, under conditions where no easy quid pro quo for such surplus is available."

In the normal case, outlined above, the investable surplus is initially generated in the agricultural sector. Gradually, however, as the manufacturing sector grows, the existence of unlimited supplies of labor ensures that sources of further manufacturing expansion are generated as profits in the manufacturing sector itself. Alternatively, in the case when the agricultural sector is incapable of generating sufficient investable funds, these may be provided by foreign capital. Again, however, this source should eventually be replaced by industrially generated profits. The only significant difference between this case and that above, is that whereas in the former, the government is required to stimulate agricultural production by means of price and tax policies, in the latter the government should encourage foreign investment in the manufacturing sector by the proper application of tax holidays and other incentives.

This suggests that the failure of an economy to accomplish industrialization may be due to either the failure to provide the manufacturing sector with sufficiently favorable terms for the purchase of food, or the inadequate generation and/or transfer of investable funds to the manufacturing sector. For an economy with Jamaica's characteristics, the problem is accentuated by the fact that the agricultural sector might not be able to generate the necessary funds. Hence, the only solution would seem to be to import such funds.

JAMAICA'S DEVELOPMENT STRATEGY

Following the experience in Puerto Rico after the Second World War, several Caribbean countries implemented their own versions of the "Operation Bootstrap." Specifically, Jamaica's strategy was heavily influenced by Arthur Lewis' studies, subsequently published by the Caribbean Commission.[3] In brief, Lewis' suggestions were as follows.

The most pressing problem in Jamaica after the Second World War was unemployment. The agricultural sector could for two reasons not be relied on to absorb the redundant labor force: first, because of agriculture's character as a labor reservoir; second, because of the necessity of (labor saving) technical change in sugar cultivation. To alleviate surplus labor in agriculture and to increase the share of the labor force productively employed, the manufacturing sector had to expand. Lewis (1950b) recognised two problems in this industrialization process: first, the sources of investable capital; second, the markets for the manufacturing output.

The first problem, according to Lewis, was to be solved by facilitating foreign investments. To accomplish this objective, the government should, first, establish an Industrial Development Corporation, which should assist foreign investors; second, implement "a battery of incentive legislation to encourage export industries in particular, but others as well" (Bernal et al. 1984, 19); and third, keep industrial wages low and maintain favorable terms of trade for the industrial sector.

The second problem arises from the small size of the domestic markets in the Caribbean. According to Lewis, it is probable that the optimal output of the manufacturing sector is larger than what could be absorbed domestically. Hence, Lewis' industrialization strategy involves export of manufactured goods from, and import of food and other agricultural goods to, the Caribbean countries.

Given the high labor-capital ratio in these countries, Lewis' suggestion appears at the surface to contradict the rules of comparative advantage. However, by taking the scarcity of land into consideration and by applying a variant of the infant industry argument, it is not very difficult to show that "the law of Comparative Costs is as valid in countries with surplus labor as in others. But whereas in the latter it is a valid foundation of arguments for free trade, in the former it is an equally valid foundation of arguments for protection" (Lewis 1954, 191). Industrialization in the Caribbean, therefore, should continue along lines involving foreign capital and import substitution.

How, then, has investment in Jamaica been financed? Table 5.1 provides a summary of some important data

The pattern is quite clear. The investment ratio increased up to about 1970 and declined thereafter. Given the rule of thumb as developed in the 1950s by Lewis and Rostow,[4] the Jamaican investment ratio is high enough to bring about self-sustained growth. Private savings as a share of domestic investment declined during the entire period as did public savings. An increasing share was thus financed out of foreign pockets.

The growing budgetary deficit can be explained by reference to government policy. During the entire 1970s, a wide-ranging (and expensive) industrial incentives program was in operation. Combining the costs of this program with the inability to exploit new sources of revenue, it follows that a budget deficit was more or less inevitable and may, in fact, have been part of the industrialization strategy.

Table 5.1
The Financing of Investment and the Pattern of Domestic Savings:
Jamaica, 1962-84. Annual Averages.
(Share of Gross Investment Except as Indicated)

Year	(1) Gross Investment J$ million, 1975 Prices	(2) Private Savings	(3) Public Savings	(4) Capital Inflow	(5) (1)/GDP
1962-66	114.0	0.786	0.100	—0.257	0.199
1967-71	285.5	0.424	0.141	0.155	0.281
1972-76	469.9	0.281	0.094	0.291	0.226
1977-81	456.0	0.252	—0.150	0.273	0.150
1980-84	1,235.5	0.199	—0.181	0.490	0.188

Sources: 1962-68: Jefferson (1971, Tables 3.1, 9.1 and 9.4); 1969: AAS (1969, Tables 74 and 76); 1970-73: NIP (1981, Accounts I, III and V); 1974-84: NIP (1984, Accounts I, III and V).
Note: Public savings equal the surplus on the current account. Net capital inflow is calculated residually.

The behavior of private savings is less obvious. During the 1960s and the first years of the 1970s, per capita incomes in Jamaica increased at the rather respectable rate of 5 percent per annum at constant prices (Danielson 1993, 108-113). According to simple Keynesian theory, this would also increase savings per capita, since consumption is related to disposable income and savings become a residual that is also related to income: as long as the level of consumption is determined by the level of income, savings, too, are determined by the level of income.[5]

This, however, seems not to be the case in Jamaica. Using the data in Table 5.1, normalized to 1975 prices, the simple Keynesian savings function for 1962-84 turns out to be

$$(5.1) \qquad H_{pr} = 428.659 - 0.1143 Y^D \qquad R^2 = 0.139$$
$$\qquad\qquad (3.026) \; (-1.84) \qquad\qquad DW = 0.85$$

where Y^D is private disposable income, H_{pr} is private (i.e., corporate plus personal), domestic savings and t-values are in parentheses.

Although the Durbin-Watson coefficient (DW) suggests the presence of auto-correlation (which is probably due to the omission of explanatory variables), it is quite clear that private savings behavior in Jamaica is not what would have been suggested by theory. One possible explanation for this is that since H_{pr} in (5.1) includes savings out of wages as well as out of profits, and since the propensity to save out of the latter often exceeds that out of the former (see below), changes in total savings may be negatively related to

Table 5.2
Gross Domestic Product by Distributive Shares.
Jamaica, 1962-84. Annual Averages.

Years	Wages	Profits	Capital Consumption	Net Indirect Taxes
1962-66	0.515	0.327	0.066	0.092
1967-71	0.483	0.330	0.097	0.091
1972-77	0.546	0.272	0.095	0.087
1978-81	0.525	0.301	0.092	0.082
1980-84	0.525	0.287	0.092	0.095

Sources: 1962-66: AAS (1968, 76); 1967-69: SBA (1973, 30); 1970-73: NIP (1981, 2); 1974-84: NIP (1984, 2-3).

changes in disposable income if the distribution of income shifts continuously in favor of wages.

As can be seen from Table 5.2, some changes in the functional distribution of income in favor of wages have taken place, although the shift is not as large as might have been expected from the regression result. It can therefore be concluded that private savings in Jamaica are probably partly governed by factors outside the scope of this analysis, such as international consumption behavior or the attitude of the government toward the private sector (or at least what the private sector thinks is the government's attitude). For instance, the consumption function can be thought of as continuously shifting upward due to demonstration effects, fear of inflation and so on.[6] Another possible explanation is that savings are related to total income only insofar as total income is related to the surplus. This issue is discussed later.

The figures in Table 5.2 should be interpreted with care. First, "wages" include labor income out of non-corporate enterprises. Because this form of enterprise becomes less important in later phases of the period, the "true" wage income (i.e., the payment to labor, excluding payment for risk-taking or entrepreneurship), may have increased more than the table indicates. Jefferson (1971, 222), in discussing similar data for the period 1950-68, however, states that "it seems unlikely ... that movements in the imputed labor income of own-account workers would seriously affect the trend displayed by wages and salaries."

Second, the item "profits" equals the operating surplus of the firm, that is, retained profits net of depreciation. Before the implementation of the bauxite industry levy of 1974, the mining industry practiced transfer pricing to some extent. Consequently, profits were probably higher before 1974 than is indicated by the table. Hence, the increase of profits' share of gross domestic income recorded for the 1978-81 period as compared to the 1971-76 period is probably an exaggeration since the figure contains profits that previously had been invisibly transferred abroad.

Table 5.3
Production and Incomes in Jamaica.

Sector	1962	1973	1984
Agriculture[a]	19.3	7.4	5.6
Mining	2.2	8.6	8.8
Manufacturing	12.6	16.5	17.8
Construction	8.7	10.2	9.0
Public Administration	6.5[b]	10.7	12.0
Distribution	15.6	20.1	20.5
GDP (J$ million, 1980 Prices)	1,561.5	2,730.0	2,323.4
GDP Per capita (J$, 1980 Prices)	940.7	1,385.8	1,010.2

Sources: AAS (1963, 42); NIP (1981, 18); NIP (1984, 23); IMF (1986, 416-417).
[a] Include forestry and fishing.
[b] The sum of Public Utilities and Public Administration.

In summary, the Jamaican development strategy focused on the hypothesis that the domestic agricultural sector was too small to accomplish the two things necessary for successful development: provide investable funds for the budding manufacturing sector and serve as a market for manufacturing goods. The solution was foreign capital and a trade policy that favored export of manufactures. However, as is demonstrated in Table 5.3, the strategy for growth and development in Jamaica does not seem to have been altogether successful—particularly not during the 1970s: per capita incomes in fixed prices fell by more than 25 percent between 1973 and 1984 and the performance of the manufacturing sector deteriorated rapidly during the same period.[7]

What is the reason for this sluggish performance? Some writers, for example Kaufman (1985) and Girvan et al. (1980), attribute it to external factors: the activities of the Intrnational Monetary Fund (IMF), the international depression following the oil crisis of 1973-74 and so on. It will be argued in this and two following chapters that an analysis of surplus in the Jamaican economy suggests that the causes of economic stagnation were primarily *domestic*; that in particular the behavior of the government explains why the success story of the 1960s was turned into virtual disaster in the 1970s.

SURPLUS IN JAMAICA, 1962-84

Recall from Chapter 3 that surplus in general is defined as net domestic product less subsistence wages, the latter being defined as the average agricultural wage. Depending on the issues at hand, different versions of the surplus may be specified. In particular, it is possible to distinguish between "productive" and "unproductive" activities by recognizing that virtually all government activities are financed out of tax revenue (i.e., out of surplus accruing to the government) and that all private activities can be assumed to generate profits.

In Table 5.4, a number of different estimates of the surplus are presented. Recall from Chapter 3 that the size of Surplus I equals the size of Surplus II and is smaller than Surplus III. Also, surplus per worker in the private sector necessarily exceeds surplus per worker when calculated for the entire employed labor force, since the contribution to GDP of labor in the public administration equals the cost of their wages.

First, Surplus I—as a share of net domestic product—has increased from some 78 percent to 83 percent during the period under study. The most significant increase in the surplus' share of the national product takes place in the 1960s (see the detailed data in Danielson 1990, Table 1). Similarly, Surplus III has increased at about the same pace, suggesting that the relative sizes of the private and the public sectors have remained virtually constant. As Michael Manley's first PNP government (1972-76) is often associated with increased public involvement in the economy and growing public sector, this result may appear somewhat surprising. It should not be, however, bearing in mind the relatively rapid growth of the Jamaican economy during the early years of the 1970s: the results of Table 5.4 simply indicate that the *relative* size of the public sector did not increase during the period (although its importance did; cf. Stephens and Stephens 1986).

Paul Baran (1957, Ch. 3)—the father of modern, empirically oriented surplus studies—has suggested that the surplus increases as per capita income increases.[8] Although Baran's definition of surplus differs substantially from that employed in this book, Baran's hypothesis merits some comments from the point of view of the present analysis. The surplus tends to increase, according to Baran, because of an increase in the degree of monopoly capitalism. This is reflected in (a) a declining share of the labor force being allocated to

Table 5.4
Size of Surplus in Jamaica, 1962-84.
Annual Averages. J$, 1975 Prices.

Years	Share of Surplus I in NDP	Share of Surplus III in NDP	Surplus per Worker, Private	Surplus per Worker, Total
1962-66	0.78	0.77	2,084	1,844
1967-71	0.82	0.81	2,827	2,530
1972-76	0.82	0.81	3,575	3,010
1977-81	0.83	0.81	3,239	2,693
1982-84	0.83	0.82	3,040	2,595

Sources: 1962-68: Jefferson (1971, Tables 3.1, 9.1 and 9.4); 1969: AAS (1969, Tables 74 and 76); 1970-73: NIP (1981, Accounts I, III and V); 1974-84: NIP (1984, Accounts I, III and V). Employment data for 1962-71: AAS (1971, Table 17); 1972-80: RLF (1980, pp.3-4); 1981-84: RLF (1984, 2-4).

productive work and the productivity of these workers increasing faster than their wages; and (b) increasing degrees of monopoly and monopsony on product and factor markets, respectively. Since Baran defines surplus as total output net of depreciation and wages to productive workers, it follows that the surplus increases.

Although the surplus as share of net domestic product increased in Jamaica during the 1960s, this is not necessarily a sign of increasing monopoly capitalism. Since the surplus is defined with labor incomes in agriculture as the base, an increasing surplus may simply be a reflection of increasing intersectoral productivity discrepancies. If average labor productivity in agriculture lags behind labor productivity in the rest of the economy, and if this lag is increasing, total surplus will increase. There is evidence that this has happened in Jamaica. In 1968, the average worker in non-agriculture produced about 4.7 times as much per annum as did the average agricultural worker; by 1984, this factor had increased to 8.7.[9]

The disintegration of the Jamaican economy is reflected in (and, to some extent, caused by) increasing intersectoral productivity discrepancies. Note in Table 5.5 that surplus per worker in the private sector both decreased at a slower rate and increased more rapidly than GDP. Total surplus per worker, on the other hand, followed the trend of GDP fairly closely. These two observations suggest that growth (as manifested by increases of per capita GDP) is largely confined to the growth center, and that negative growth of GDP severely affected agricultural wages. Since surplus per worker in the private sector did not decline as much as GDP, subsistence earnings also declined; and as surplus per worker in the private sector increased faster than GDP, it follows that wage levels in the agricultural sector lagged behind.

In the simple model of a dual economy developed by Lewis (1954)—a model that is a modified version of the one-sector Ricardian model discussed in Chapter 2— resources are transferred from the traditional to the modern sector where part of the resources goes to labor in the form of higher wages and part goes to capitalists in the form of profits and (possibly) part goes to the government in the form of tax revenue. According to the classical assumptions employed by Lewis, workers do not save and capitalists save a substantial

Table 5.5
Growth of Income and Surplus in Jamaica.
Percent. Average Annual Rates. 1975 Prices.

Period	GDP	GDP per capita	Surplus per Worker, Private	Surplus per Worker, Total
1962-73	7.4	5.1	8.3	7.5
1974-84	-1.9	-2.8	-0.9	-1.1
1962-84	2.0	0.3	3.2	2.9

Sources: AAS (1963, 42); NIP (1981, 18); NIP (1984, 23); IMF (1986, 416-417).

amount of their profits (in the simplest case, capitalists save their entire income). If these assumptions are relevant for Jamaica, it should thus be expected to find a positive correlation between capitalists' share of the surplus and the domestic savings ratio.

Table 5.6 demonstrates the shares of Surpluses I, II and III accruing to the private sector (i.e., as excess wages and profits); the remainder accrues to the government in the form of net indirect taxes and, for S_{II} and S_{III}, direct taxes.

The private share of Surplus I—that is, the sum of excess wages and profits as percentage of total Surplus I—hovers between 88 and 91 percent. The private shares of S_{II} and S_{III} show a similar behavior, although of course the private share of S_{II} is smaller than the private share of S_I and the private shares for both S_{II} and S_{III} decline over time, whereas such a trend cannot be discerned for the private share of S_I. This is, as shown in Chapter 3, because the private shares of Surpluses II and III are defined net of income taxes, whereas the private share of Surplus I is defined gross of income taxes. Consequently, the difference in the trend for S_I in relation to the trends for S_{II} and S_{III} can be attributed to increasing tax burdens being levied on labor and capitalists. Similarly, the private share of S_{II} is smaller than the private share of S_{III}. This is because the latter is defined to include the costs of all public employees in the surplus (all public sector employment is defined as unproductive and hence financed out of the surplus). This part of the surplus come in the form of wages, so labor's share of Surplus III is necessarily larger than labor's share of Surplus II. Finally, the private share of S_I is somewhat larger than the private share of S_{III}. Since income taxes are excluded from the private share of the latter while public expenditures on employment are defined as surplus, this suggests that the government consistently has spent more resources on public sector employment than it has managed to extract in the form of tax revenue. As Danielson (1993, 151-161), shows this is a correct interpretation with the proviso that Jamaican governments (and in particular the PNP government) did not increase employment only by directly increasing wage payments, but by increasing subsidies to parts of the service sector as well.[10]

Table 5.6
The Functional Distribution of the Surplus:
Jamaica, 1962-84. Annual Averages.

Period	Surplus I		Surplus II		Surplus III	
	Wages	Profits	Wages	Profits	Wages	Profits
1962-66	0.41	0.47	0.39	0.37	0.42	0.39
1967-71	0.47	0.44	0.45	0.35	0.42	0.38
1972-76	0.56	0.33	0.50	0.25	0.51	0.29
1977-81	0.54	0.36	0.47	0.25	0.47	0.26
1982-84	0.55	0.33	0.47	0.26	0.47	0.30

Sources: AAS (1963, 42); NIP (1981, 18); NIP (1984, 23); IMF (1986, 416-417).

Turning now to the distribution of the private share of the surpluses it is quite clear that the functional distribution of the surplus has been turned in favor of excess wages. For Surplus I, labor received, in the form of excess wages, approximately 40 percent of the total surplus product in the early 1960s; this share had increased to 55 percent in the early 1980s. As can also be noted from the table, this shift in the distribution of surplus has taken place at the expense of profits: capitalists' share of Surplus I fell from almost 50 percent in the early 1960s to only a third in the early 1980s. The pattern is similar for S_{II} and S_{III}. In particular, the data for Surplus III is interesting in this regard. Since the government extracts income taxes from labor as well as from capitalists and uses that revenue to employ—directly or indirectly—labor, the government's fiscal behavior is in effect a redistribution of surplus from capitalists to labor. To what extent this is a conscious strategy or an unintended side effect of the government's policy is an issue that will be discussed in Chapter 7.

The pattern that emerges from Table 5.6 is thus one in which an increasing share of the surplus is being distributed to labor in the form of "excess" wages. Since the public shares of Surpluses II and III increase during the period, it can be concluded that incomes have been redistributed from capitalists to laborers. This may appear as contradictory to policies. Edward Seaga, who succeeded Manley as Prime Minister in 1980, promised a return to market oriented strategies—far away from Manley's allegedly socialist development strategy. Two of Seaga's prime goals were deregulation of the economy (which essentially meant less state involvement in business) and emphasis on private initiative (for which improved opportunities to make private profits were strategic).[11]

Table 5.6 gives no indication of Seaga's success in this matter. On the contrary, the table demonstrates that (a) the share of profits declined between 1977-81 and 1982-84 and (b) that the public share of the surplus increased between the same periods. If anything, the results indicate that developments in Jamaica during Seaga's first four years followed the same path as Seaga claimed were driving Jamaica bankrupt during the PNP period: increased wages at the expense of private profitability and increased government involvement at the expense of the private initiative.

CONCLUDING REMARKS

The structural changes accompanying a secular rise in per capita incomes in developing economies have apparently not been present in Jamaica during the period of study. This may be partly because incomes were stagnant over a number of years, although not even in the 1960s—a period during which per capita incomes in volume terms increased at an annual rate of more than 5 percent; see Table 5.2—did the expected structural changes occur. In fact, manufacturing output as a share of GDP declined from 14 percent at Independence to 13 percent ten years later. Moreover, the share of the primary sector in GDP decreased from 22 percent in 1962 to some 19 percent in 1973. Thus, the Jamaican economy is a virtual service economy. In 1984, the tertiary sector accounted for some 55 percent of total value added; and within this sector the dominant areas were distribution and production of government services.

Why has there been no change in economic structures as in many other countries? Has Jamaica been suffering from "eurosclerosis"? Some possible (and tentative) answers can be suggested.

First, the size of the surplus emanates from the large sectoral productivity discrepancies between agriculture and the rest of the economy, discrepancies that are accentuated by the rather special character of the mining sector. A stagnant agricultural sector acts as a brake on the entire system: given a small, densely populated economy, the choice for the government is not between promotion of agriculture and promotion of industry. The two are complementary; and it is virtually impossible to accomplish, say, a successful industrialization if not the productivity of the agricultural workers is increasing at the same time.[12]

Second, one of the major lessons from Arthur Lewis' (1954) unlimited labor article is that industrialization usually is financed out of saved profits. With surplus labor, the share of profits in national income increases as the modern sector expands. This increases national savings and thus provides the funds for further industrialization. Lewis' conclusion has sometimes mistakenly been taken for a recommendation: that the government *should*—to increase the rate of industrialization—turn the distribution of income in favor of profits. Commenting on the reception of his 1954 article, Lewis (1984, 134) remarks: "I was frequently attacked for recommending this change in income distribution, but I was not making recommendations; I was trying to understand, not to prescribe. This was not specifically a capitalist answer, since the same answer could be reached for the USSR, with the profits of the state firm and the turnover tax performing the same function as the sources of increased savings."

It is shown in this chapter that the aggregate, private savings propensity in Jamaica is not particularly encouraging: private savings as a share of national income is actually declining. It is, however, also demonstrated that surplus income has been redistributed away from capitalists. This means that the capitalists' share of the total surplus has declined. As seen in Chapter 2, falling profits in classical theory means falling investments since it is capitalists who are the most important savers and investors in the economy. Since this indicates that the share of profits in national income has declined, the result does not contradict Lewis' observation.

Finally, it has been shown that the deteriorating private savings behavior has not been accompanied by any significant savings on the part of the state. Indeed, as Table 5.1 clearly demonstrates, public savings (i.e., the excess of tax revenues over current expenditures) as share of total investments has fallen from the late 1960s and been negative since the mid-1970s. Consequently, Jamaica has had to rely on importation of foreign capital to finance investments. Although this is perfectly in line with Arthur Lewis' recommendations and the strategy adopted by several other Caribbean countries (including Puerto Rico in the famous Operation Bootstrap), there are reasons to suspect that a heavy reliance on foreign capital does not speed up the structural transformations necessary for self-sustained growth. One of these reasons—which is minutely scrutinised in the study by Norman Girvan (1970)—is that foreign investments tend to exploit profitable opportunities created by the existing structure. If domestic resources to exploit these opportunities are lacking, foreign capital may be a blessing. But reliance on foreign capital may also lead to the failure to create an appropriate domestic capital market and to a neglect of the structural changes necessary to create new profitable opportunities in other sectors of the economy. This, in turn, may create an attitude among domestic agents that promotes neither domestic savings nor risk-taking and entrepreneurship.

The increasing surplus found in the analysis is not necessarily a sign of increasing "monopoly capitalism." It seems that the surplus increases because sectoral productivity discrepancies increase. This, in turn, suggests that economic growth in Jamaica has been concentrated to a few sectors with relatively insignificant trickle down effects. The economy is thus becoming increasingly polarized and that an increasing share of the population becomes marginalized due to the capital-intensive nature of economic growth. Marginalization implies that the *personal* distribution of income deteriorates. Apparently, this has not stimulated savings. Given the increasing imports of consumer goods and of capital goods for personal use, it may be suggested that the upper deciles' increasing incomes have been allocated mainly to consumption of imported goods. This hypothesis is the theme of Chapter 6.

The causes of Jamaica's stagnation are not to be found in lack of resources. Even if the particular definition of "subsistence" developed here is considered parsimonious, the fact remains that the surplus has increased during the period 1962-84. The causes of stagnation are rather to be sought in either the deteriorating savings behavior or in the apparent lack of dynamism in the economy. Although the latter has not been considered in detail in this chapter,[13] it is quite clear that a large share of foreign capital may hinder structural change and thus prevent Jamaica from adapting optimally to changing international conditions. Insofar as investment is important for growth and development, and to the extent that large inflows of foreign capital may arrest structural change, it is quite clear that self-sustained growth in Jamaica demands better domestic savings performance. Unless some domestic income recipients can be persuaded to live a less riotous life, such savings must be generated within the public sector.

APPENDIX TO CHAPTER 5: SOURCES AND QUALITY OF DATA

This short Appendix briefly describes (i) the sources of data material utilized and (ii) the methods used for creation of unavailable material. Since a major point in this book is that the approach devised utilizes only easily accessible data, that is, data from the national accounts, it is important that the transformation method is correctly described. Hence the need for the Appendix.

Most of the material is taken from the annual *National Income and Product*, published by Kingston's Statistical Institute. This material is reproduced in a number of summary publications, such as the *Statistical Yearbook* and the *Annual Abstract of Statistics*. Much of the material is subject to repeated revisions; attempts were made to use the latest revision available.

The data material is not of perfect quality. First, Gross Domestic Product in purchases' values does not always turn out to be the sum of Compensation to Employees, Operating Surplus, Capital Consumption and Net Indirect Taxes. To avoid invisible errors, GDP is defined here as the sum of these magnitudes. This approach may be questionable, but it does have the advantage of making the shares of surplus add to unity.

Second, for some years during the 1960s, data on employment simply does not exist. Specifically, this is true for data on sectoral employment for the period 1962 to 1968. It is possible to find indications of change in the employment structure by looking at the Employment Surveys (reported in the *Annual Abstract of Statistics*); some estimates are also found in the German publication *Länderkurzberichte: Jamaika*, published by the Statistical Institute in Wiesbaden, FRG. In the 1973 issue of that publication a few estimates of sectoral employment are reported. Since data material on per capita wages in agriculture is strategic to this method, and since data on agricultural wages are reported on an aggregate basis in the national accounts, it is important to have information concerning agricultural employment. It is assumed here that the rate of change in the employment structure during the years for which employment data are unavailable is constant. Hence, if employment is known in the year t and in the year $t+3$, employment in $t+1$, L_{t+1}, is estimated as

(A5.1) $$L_{t+1} = L_t + \frac{L_{t+3} - L_t}{3}.$$

If this assumption for some reason appears implausible, the reader is advised to concentrate on the period 1969-84: here, the statistical series are complete.

The estimates in the tables are made by using data from the *National Income and Product Accounts* for the period 1969-84; for the period 1962-68 data from the *Annual Abstract of Statistics* is used in most cases. Data on sectoral wage payments for 1962-69 can be found in *National Income and Product, 1970*; for 1970-73 in *National Income and Product, 1981*, and for 1974-84 in *National Income and Product, 1984*. These data have been complemented by data from the following sources: *Jamaika: Länderkurzberichte, 1973*, Wiesbaden, FRG: Statistische Bundesamt, pp.17-18 (employment); *Statistical Abstract*, 1974-82, Section II, Kingston: Statistical Institute (employment); *International Financial Statistics, Yearbook, 1986*, Washington, DC: International Monetary Fund, pp. 416-417 (gross investment and implicit GDP deflator); *Report on the Labour Force, 1972*, Kingston: Department of Statistics, 1973 (employment); *Consumer Price Indices*, various issues, Kingston: Statistical Institute (price indices).

Finally, all data on agricultural magnitudes have been deflated to urban price levels using price indices in the mentioned *Consumer Price Indices*.

NOTES

1. For additional details, see Danielson (1993, Chs. 4-6).

2. Wyn Owen (1966) notes that the agricultural sector is exposed to a "double developmental squeeze" during socialist as well as during capitalist development. The squeeze, which is a combination of income redistribution and production transfer, is—during socialist development—attained by using various extraction methods, such as taxes, fees and outright confiscation. Capitalist development has, according to Owen, displayed a similar pattern, since the combination of competition and rapid technical change in agriculture implies, first, continuous resource reallocation away from agriculture and, second, deteriorating terms of trade for agriculture. A further discussion of Owen's ideas can be found in Chapter 4.

3. Lewis (1944) is a critique of the Economic Policy Committee's plan; Lewis (1950a) and (1950b) are, respectively, an analysis of the Puerto Rican experience and an analysis of the prospects for industrialisation in the British West Indies. Further details are provided by Jefferson (1971).

4. That is, that self-sustained growth requires an increase of the savings ratio from below 5 percent to over 10 percent.

5. Due to lack of reliable data for many poor countries, available estimates of savings functions are of varying quality. See, however, Mikesell and Zinser (1973) who survey the available material and find the marginal propensity to save to be positive in most cases. A word of warning is issued by Snyder (1974, 140) according to whom the average propensity to save "is particularly erratic in developing countries, many of

which are undergoing rapid structural changes plus evolution in attitudes towards work, consumption and thrift."

6. Danielson (1993, Ch. 6) argues that such factors are important for understanding the behavior of public expenditures in Jamaica.

7. A detailed analysis of the manufacturing sector in the 1960s and 1970s is provided by Ayub (1981) who also discusses the system of incentives for that sector.

8. Baran's hypothesis, although originally formulated in 1957 was not subjected to any systematic tests until 1966 when Joseph D. Phillips (1966) made an attempt to calculate the surplus for the United States for the period 1929 to 1963. Phillips' findings basically confirmed Baran's hypothesis. However, Phillips' approach has been criticized for some weaknesses, including double-counting of profit income. See the discussion in Dawson and Foster (1992) where also the U.S. surplus is calculated for the period 1963-88. Baran's increasing surplus hypothesis is discussed and criticized in several of the essays in Davis (1992), including Lippit (1992), Stanfield (1992) and Fishman (1992).

9. Jefferson (1971, 281); the 1984 figure is calculated from information in *Statistical Abstract* (1984, Tables 2.2 and 15.3). This information is also evidence for huge inequalities in the personal distribution of income.

10. The phenomenon of increasing subsidies is no small matter. Total government subsidies in 1980 prices increased from J$33.6 million in 1970 to J$277.3 million in 1978 and to J$652.9 million in 1981. Of these, the share allocated to the service sector and to other industries wholly or partly controlled by the government increased during the 1970s, reaching a peak of 92 percent in 1980 (Danielson 1993, Table 6.7). Chapter 7 discusses this phenomenon in more detail.

11. See Stephens and Stephens (1986, Ch. 7) for an account of Seaga's "economic model" and ibid. (Chs. 4-6) for an account of PNP's policies and Seaga's (and others) criticism.

12. "It is not the case that agriculture cannot continue to develop if industry is developed. Exactly the opposite is true: agriculture cannot be put on a basis where it will yield a reasonable standard of living unless new jobs are created off land" (Lewis 1950b, par. 21).

13. See Ayub (1981, Ch. 3), Danielson (1986, Ch. 4) or Girvan et al. (1980) for detailed analyses of the relations between dynamism and foreign capital.

6

Mechanisms of Stagnation

The definition of surplus, as developed in Chapter 3, was calculated for Jamaica in the preceding chapter. It was shown there that the surplus—measured as Surplus II or Surplus III—increased significantly during the 1960s and 1970s (cf. Table 5.4). One possible explanation for this would be the Baran (1957) hypothesis of an increasing degree of monopoly capitalism. According to this hypothesis, the surplus increases as per capita incomes grow because markets (for commodities as well as for factors of production) become distinguished by increasing imperfections—monopoly on commodity markets and monopsony on factor markets. In addition, economic growth, according to Baran is, more often than not, characterized by a declining share of the employed labor force working in productive (i.e., surplus-generating) activities and the gap between the productivity and the wage of the productive labor force widens. Hence, according to Baran, increasing monopoly capitalism occurs when per capita incomes increase and this is reflected, inter alia, in an increasing share of the surplus being allocated to capitalists in the form of increasing profits.

However, in Jamaica profits fell more or less consistently between the late 1960s and the early 1980s,[1] which would not seem to indicate any increase in the degree of monopoly capitalism (at least not in Baran's sense). Furthermore, as noted in Chapter 5, the relatively rapid increase for most years of the 1960s of per capita incomes as well as of profits was in the 1970s turned into a deep and long recession. Per capita incomes—and for some years, even GDP—fell while the functional shares of GDP remained virtually constant, thus indicating that different classes in society carried their part of the burden of stagnation. One of the major points of Chapter 5, however, was that profits *as share of Surplus II and Surplus III* declined systematically throughout the 1970s: as Table 5.4 shows, the share of profits in Surplus III declined from approximately 39 percent in 1962-66 to 26 percent in 1977-81. This phenomenon was manifested in an increasing wage share as well as in an increasing share of the surplus accruing to the government. Chapter 5 also noted that the 1970s were characterized by a deteriorating savings behavior—on the part of private actors as well as the government. It would seem natural to assume savings to decline as per capita incomes fall; however, it was demonstrated that no significant relation existed between these two variables (see equation 5.1).

To pursue the point further, note with Danielson (1993, Fig. 4.3) that the average propensity to save for private agents (i.e., workers and private capitalists) fell from a respectable 14 percent of GDP in the early 1960s to an all-time low of less than 1 percent of GDP in 1976. These facts point to the conclusion that the stagnation encountered during the 1970s and early 1980s was correlated to the volume of surplus being allocated to consumption or, as it were, "unproductive" uses. However, the issue concerning the workings of the mechanisms leading, first, to an increasing share of surplus being consumed and, second, from surplus disposal to economic growth (or failure thereof) has not yet been considered.

The purpose of this chapter is to offer further vindication of this particular story of Jamaica's stagnation and to suggest that the key to an understanding of Jamaica's failure of attaining economic growth in the 1970s lies in the government's economic policies and its consequential effects on the distribution of the surplus. The Appendix presents some results for an intenational data set.

CLASSICAL ECONOMIC GROWTH

As discussed in some detail in Chapter 2, the classical mechanism of economic growth relies on the size and distribution of the surplus. Here, surplus is defined as that part of the annual product that is not necessary for replication of last year's production this year. The *size* of the surplus thus depends primarily on the size and productivity of surplus-generating activities. Further, the surplus is distributed between different groups. The mechanisms governing that distribution is of no concern now—it is discussed in Chapter 6—but it should be emphasized that as long as different classes or surplus-receiving groups dispose of the surplus in different ways, the distribution of the surplus will be decisive for the rate of economic growth. As a simple example, recall the Ricardian one-sector model of Chapter 2 in which landlords consume all of their income unproductively while capitalists invest all their income in surplus-generating activities. Given the size of the surplus, the rate of growth of the economy will in this example be higher the larger the share of surplus being appropriated by the latter class.

In terms of post-war development economics, Arthur Lewis' (1954) dual economy model mimics the classical growth mechanism quite closely. If small-scale agriculture is characterized by a high level of disguised unemployment, sustained economic expansion will be associated with (a) a transfer of labor from agriculture to other *private* sectors in the economy and (b) an increasing share of the surplus accruing as profits. This mechanism relies on the assumption that the supply schedule of labor that private, non-agricultural firms meet is highly, and in the limit infinitely, elastic. If the share of profits does not increase—either because the expansion takes place in state-owned enterprises or because the increasing profits are taxed away—an additional condition must be fulfilled if sustained economic expansion is to be attained: the public sector must save a large part of its surplus income. It is not necessary to make that assumption regarding private firms since profits (as defined in the GDP identity) are net of capital consumption and the major part of profits is consequently saved (either at home or abroad).

The similarity between classical growth theory and the Lewisian dual economy model is clearly spelled out by Lewis (1972, 448) in a clarification of the original model: "The reason why savings are low in underdeveloped countries relatively to national income is not that people are poor but that capitalist profits are low relatively to national income. As the capitalist sector expands, profits grow relatively and an increasing proportion of national income is reinvested."

This mechanism—which is the central piece of dual economic development á la Lewis—assumes, first, that the capitalist sector faces "unlimited" supplies of labor and, second, that capitalists have a higher-than-average propensity to save. In the presented definitions of surplus, Lewis' first assumption is not necessary. Following the definition of S_{III} (equation 3.5), the very existence of a surplus accruing to labor is the sign of (a) skill premiums paid to non-agricultural labor; (b) the existence of monopolistic elements in the non-agricultural labor markets; and/or (c) an upward-sloping labor supply curve facing the non-agricultural producers. In any case, the critical assumption to make is than concerning the relative savings propensities for labor and capitalists: if the latter group saves relatively more than the former, the share of the surplus accruing to capitalists will be positively correlated to the volume of private savings in the economy, and vice versa. As seen in Chapter 5, the distribution of surplus in Jamaica has changed noticeably during the period under study (1962-84) and it will be argued that this has fundamentally altered the prospects for sustained economic growth.

SAVINGS, INVESTMENTS AND THE DISTRIBUTION OF SURPLUS

Provided that GDP per capita in real prices is taken as an indicator of economic growth, it is well known that economic growth in Jamaica ceased about the time when Manley's PNP assumed power in 1972 (cf. Table 5.3). Between 1962 and 1973 per capita incomes grew, in 1975 prices, from J$940 to J$1,386 or, by approximately 4.3 percent per annum. In 1984 per capita incomes had fallen to some J$1,000 per annum or, by approximately 2.5 percent per annum. This means that the per capita income in 1984 was only some 70 percent of per capita income 11 years earlier.[2] Now, many factors may have contributed to Jamaica's stagnation: the international recession following the oil-price boom of 1973 slowed down import demand in North America and in Europe; that the PNP assumed power may have prevented potential investors from putting their money into Jamaican businesses; the activities of the opposition (local as well as foreign) slowed down economic growth, in particular of the tourist industry; and so forth. There is, however, little if any evidence that these factors actually contributed to the abnormally long period of stagnation in the country. What is seldom appreciated in the literature is that the tax and expenditure policies devised by the PNP government fundamentally altered the distribution of the surplus.[3] As will be argued, this was one of the major factors causing the cessation of economic growth and the explanation makes perfect sense in the light of classical economic theory.

One of the distinguishing features of the first Manley government (i.e., between 1972 and 1976) was the rapid expansion of public activities, in terms of revenues as well as expenditures. Between the two elections of 1972 and 1976, total public expenditures increased by approximately 9 percent per annum (in fixed prices). Revenues increased by about 3 percent per annum. In healthy, growing economies these are perhaps not very startling figures. However, since per capita incomes in Jamaica, between 1972 and 1976 fell by approximately 2 percent per annum, an annual increase in government revenue of 3 percent does indeed seem very large. The share of public revenue in GDP increased from approximately 19 percent in 1972 to some 23 percent in 1976. The corresponding figures for public expenditures were 23 and 38 percent, respectively.[4]

Although these figures record total expenditures and total revenue—so capital transactions are included—the expansion was most significant for current transactions and, in the case of expenditures, consumption items. Government consumption measured in 1980 prices, for instance, increased from J$795 million in 1972 to J$1,089 million five years later or by approximately 7 percent per annum. Indeed the major part of the expansion of expenditures was dedicated to fulfil promises made during the election campaign. Although few of these policies were entirely successful, projects such as the adult literacy program, the new housing policies and the extended food subsidization program swallowed considerable amounts of money during the first years of the first PNP government.[5] Furthermore, the period saw significant increases in the government's wage bill, both because public employment expanded and because money wages increased: between 1973 and 1976 the average weekly wage in 30 public employment categories increased by 75 percent and public employment increased, between 1972 and 1977, by 46 percent (Girvan et al. 1980, Table 14; RLF 1980, 1984).

The attempts to raise revenue to meet the expanding expenditures were not entirely successful. Although the Bauxite Levy, imposed in 1974, raised government revenue by approximately 15-20 percent during the first few years after implementation, expansion of the mining sector ceased in the late 1970s so levy earnings did not come forward at the expected rate.[6] Furthermore, since GDP in fixed prices actually declined after 1973, income-elastic revenue declined as well. Consequently, the government increased in the mid-1970s its efforts to find new sources of revenue.[7] However, due to sluggish performance of production, tax revenues did not keep pace with expenditures (which, in the election year of 1976, were heavily expanded). As a result, the 1976-77 budget showed a deficit of approximately J$525 million, some 40 percent of total expenditures. Since the possibilities of commercial external lending deteriorated rapidly,[8] parts of the deficit was financed by way of note-printing. More than 50 percent of the 1976-77 deficit was financed in this manner thus putting additional fuel on the inflation fire.

Although the first Manley government did not succeed in raising sufficient revenue to cover expenditures, substantial amounts were in fact collected. As previously seen, current revenue in 1980 prices increased between 1972 and 1976 at a rate of approximately 3 percent per annum, meaning that the share of revenues in GDP increased from 19 to 23 percent. This had serious consequences for the functional distribution of the surplus. As can be seen in Table 6.1, which is a detailed exposition of part of Table 5.6, the share of Surplus III accruing as profits dropped from approximately 38 percent in 1967-71 to about 29 percent in 1972-76. As has been indicated, the larger part of this decline took place towards the end of the period—specifically after the announcement of the Bauxite Levy and the subsequent declaration of Democratic Socialism in 1974. Although the share of profits in S_{III} recovered somewhat during the following five-year period, it never again reached the levels of the 1960s. The share of surplus accruing to labor, on the other hand, increased significantly up

Table 6.1
Distribution of Surplus III.
Annual Averages. Percent.

| Period | Wages[a] | | | Net | |
	Total	Private	Public	Profits	Taxes[b]
1962-66	42	39	3	39	18
1967-71	42	38	4	38	20
1972-76	51	44	7	29	20
1977-81	47	40	7	26	27
1982-84	47	41	6	30	23

Sources: See Danielson (1990), Appendix. Data on taxes on wages and profits from Ministry of Finance: *Annual Estimates of Revenue*, various issues.
[a] Net of income taxes.
[b] Net indirect taxes plus income taxes.

to 1972-76. As has been indicated, much of this increase was due to a relatively rapid growth of money wages. Moreover, the government's expenditure policies—that included a rapid growth of social services—led to an increasing part of the labor force being employed in the public sector. As is indicated in the table, the share of S_{III} accruing to public labor increased from approximately 4 percent in the late 1960s to 7 percent in the following years.

As was argued in the beginning of this chapter, there are reasons to believe that such a significant redistribution of surplus in such a short time affects national savings. It is well known that private savings in Jamaica declined drastically during the first half of the 1970s, culminating in 1976-77 with a negative value. Furthermore, the decline of savings cannot be explained by the contraction of the volume of surplus: the average private propensity to save out of Surplus III declined from approximately 20 percent in the late 1960s to less than 5 percent in the late 1970s.[9] Any attempt to explain the variations in private, national savings must then take into account other factors than variations in the volume of surplus. It is suggested here that different income categories have different propensities to save. Specifically, the discussion here follow classical traditions by using the established post-Keynesian assumption that the propensity to save out of profits exceed that out of wage income.[10] In terms of surplus, the suggestion is that the propensity to save out of profits is higher than the propensity to save out of "excess" wages.

The hypothesis that private savings are dependent on the volume as well as the distribution of the surplus is confirmed by regression analysis. The dependent variable used is gross private savings—that is, gross national savings less the public budget surplus—in 1980 prices (H_{pr}). Explanatory variables are: the volume of S_{III} accruing to labor and capitalists, PRS_{III}; the share of PRS_{III} accruing as profits, I;[11] and time, t, to capture trends in private savings that are not related to these variables. All values have been converted into natural logarithms so the estimated coefficients can be interpreted as elasticities.[12] Using Ordinary Least Squares (OLS) over the period 1962-84, the result, with t-statistics in parentheses is as follows:[13]

$$(6.1) \quad \ln(H_{pr}) = -7.17 + 2.17\ln(PRS_{III}) + 2.64\ln(I) - 0.62t$$
$$\phantom{(6.1) \quad \ln(H_{pr}) =} (-0.99) \quad (2.08) (2.76) (-2.93)$$

$$\bar{R}^2 = 0.53 \quad DW = 2.09 \quad F_{(3,20)} = 10.35.$$

Approximately half of the variations in private savings are explained by the volume and distribution of the surplus, and a time trend. One may, of course, prefer to say that approximately half of the variations remain unexplained; however, in view of the generally poor correlation between income and savings observed in most poor countries (and not least the poor relation between income and savings in Jamaica reported in equation 5.1), this result should be considered rather promising.[14] Three of the four coefficients are significantly different from zero at a one-tailed t-test, the Durbin-Watson statistic indicates no autocorrelation and the F-statistic confirms that the included independent variables are significant for private savings.[15] The most interesting feature of the result, however, is no doubt that the elasticity of private savings with respect to private surplus as well as to the distribution of private surplus exceeds unity.[16] A 1 percent increase of the volume of private surplus, ceteris paribus, has during the period increased private savings by approximately 2.2 percent. Similarly, the regression suggests that the functional distribution of surplus is a strategic factor for the amount of national resources saved: if disposable profits increase relative to "excess" wages by 1 percent (and the total volume of private surplus is held constant) private savings have during the period on average increased by 2.6 percent.

This is the key to an understanding of the disappointing performance of national savings in Jamaica. The aggressive fiscal policies adopted by the PNP government after 1972 altered the functional distribution of surplus in favor of labor. This affected private savings negatively with severe consequences for the balance of payments and consequently for the government's room to maneuver. Profitability and consequently savings in Jamaican firms were further depressed by the rocketing of oil prices and the subsequent stagnation of demand in the industrialised countries; this is reflected in the high value of the coefficient for PRS_{III}.

THE DISTRIBUTION OF SURPLUS AND INTERNATIONAL TRADE

Is a high level of national savings really necessary for sustained economic growth? The relation between savings and investment is, of course, not as clear-cut as often seems to be the case in textbooks and one may indeed dispute the simplistic view that savings are automatically translated into productive investments that, through the multiplier, increase the GDP, a view which has been maintained since classical economics.[17] In poor countries the relations between national savings and investments are more complex. If investments are not completely financed out of national resources, the balance of payments will show a deficit. Since this is often covered by loans from abroad, repayable in foreign currency, the room for importation of capital goods, necessary for productive investments becomes limited. For Jamaica, it can be added to the picture that the government's huge and growing deficit has also been largely financed by international loans thus adding further to the foreign exchange constraint (cf. Chapter 5).

The redistribution of the discussed surplus has another side than the deteriorating savings behavior: what capitalists have lost, workers have gained and while capitalists save a good part of the surplus income, workers consume. In particular, surplus has been redistributed to wage recipients with a high propensity to consume imported goods. This has tightened the foreign exchange constraint and consequently the importation of capital goods has diminished at approximately the rate at which imports of consumer goods have increased.

This hypothesis thus consists of two parts: first, that imported capital goods constitute an essential and non-substitutable component of domestic investment and, second, that surplus incomes to an increasing degree have been expended on imported consumption goods. Consideration begins with the latter.

As was demonstrated in the previous section, the surplus has, largely because of the government's fiscal policies, been redistributed in favor of labor. All labor, however, has not gained. Although reliable data on wages in individual enterprises are difficult to come by, the available material suggests that middle- and high-income wage recipients have gained more than low-income wage recipients. Thus for instance Norman Girvan et al. (1980, 141) report that money wages increased by approximately 100 percent between 1973 and 1977. Taking inflation into account, the change in real wages was thus roughly 50 percent. During the same period, the average annual rate of *decline* of real wages in agriculture was approximately 2 percent per annum.[18] This implies two things. First, the increase in wages may be interpreted as an increase of "excess" wages, since the average annual wage—which is defined as subsistence—fell. On average real "excess" wages increased between 1973 and 1977 by 60 percent or, by approximately 10 percent per annum. Second, since agricultural labor did not enjoy an increase of real income and since the agricultural sector exhibits the lowest average wage in the economy, the personal distribution of income was turned against low-income groups. If this result is combined with the suggestion made earlier concerning the trends in the functional distribution of surplus, one arrives at a conclusion that an increasing share of the surplus was distributed to middle- and high-income wage recipients at the expense of capitalists and low-income wage recipients.[19] Further vindication is provided by an examination of the trend in the ratio of the agricultural to the economy-wide wage rate. Although the former has always been lower than the average, the trend is, for the most part of the period, negative. In the early 1960s the average agricultural wage was approximately 40 percent of the average economy-wide wage. The trend starts downwards around 1965—probably because of the expansion of the bauxite industry—and reaches a bottom of less than 20 percent in 1970 where it has remained ever since.[20]

The change in the distribution of surplus has severely affected the structure of consumption. In particular, surplus resources have been transferred to groups characterized by high propensities to consume imported goods. This observation is not novel: Michael Manley (1976, 118) addressing the growing trade deficit in the early 1970s referred to the "orgy of consumption of imported luxury goods"—a characterization that is substantiated by Owen Jefferson's (1971,

198) remark that the late 1960s and early 1970s saw a "tremendous growth in imports of consumer durables such as motor cars, refrigerators, radios and phonographs." Table 6.2 provides further evidence.

This table is based on a somewhat arbitrary classification of non-fuel imports into three economic classes: consumption goods, intermediary goods and "capital" goods. The basic objective has been to separate consumption goods from the remainder of non-fuel imports. Although imports under the Standard International Trade Classification (SITC) Sections 4 and 8 are not necessarily commodities for consumption, inspection of Jamaican data reveals that the majority of imports under these headings are olive oil, sesame oil and soy (SITC 4) and furniture, clothing and watches (SITC 8)—commodities that clearly are neither intermediate goods, nor capital goods. The group "capital" goods consists of Manufactured Goods Classified Chiefly by Material (SITC 6) and Machinery and Transport Equipment (SITC 7). Although the latter clearly should be regarded as capital goods, the former may seem a bit more ambiguous. However, the majority of goods imported under this heading seems not to be for consumption; in any case SITC 6 forms a relatively small part of total imports so its exclusion would not seriously harm the argument.

All three groups exhibit distinct trends: upward for consumption goods and intermediate goods and downward for "capital" goods. The development of capital goods imports is indeed alarming: between the early 1960s and the early 1980s, the share of these goods in total imports fell from over 40 percent to a shadow over 5 percent. The evidence thus presented paints a picture of surplus redistribution in favor of middle- and high-income wage recipients that demand imported consumption goods. Since, during the best part of the 1970s, export performance has been disappointing and debt payments have been accelerating, the room for capital goods imports has shrunk considerably (Danielson 1993, Ch. 5).

Table 6.2
Composition of Non-Fuel Imports.
Percent of Total Imports Except as Indicated. Annual Averages.

Period	Imports % of GDP	Consumption Goods[a]	Intermediate Goods[b]	"Capital" Goods[c]
1962-66	42.7	40.3	16.9	42.8
1967-71	44.8	46.3	21.0	32.7
1972-76	42.3	56.8	27.3	15.9
1977-81	47.0	58.0	31.8	10.2
1982-84	53.2	60.0	33.9	6.1

Sources: IYTS (1965, 411-2; 1969, 443-5; 1975, 432-3; 1978, 643-5); *External Trade (1983,* Table 2; *1984,* Table 2).

[a] SITC 0, 1, 4 and 8.
[b] SITC 2 and 5.
[c] SITC 6,7 and 9.

The second part of the evidence consists of demonstrating that there is a close correlation between domestic investments and capital goods imports. Although some of the commodities used for investments are produced locally—such as cement and some other building equipment—important goods conventionally associated with productive, that is, surplus-generating investments—such as machinery and vehicles—are not domestically produced and have to be imported. To examine the extent to which Jamaica is dependent on imported capital goods, gross domestic investments have been regressed against imports of SITC 7 goods (Machinery and Transport Equipment). With all values in 1980 prices and t-values in parentheses, the OLS estimate for the period 1962-84 is as follows:[21]

$$(6.2) \qquad I_d = 163.6 + 1.47M_c \quad R^2 = 0.89$$
$$\qquad\qquad (1.83) \;\; (5.39) \qquad DW = 1.41$$

where I_d is gross investments and M_c is SITC 7 imports. The result suggests a close relation between gross investments and capital goods imports. On average, about two-thirds of gross investment consist of imported capital goods (i.e., for each J\$ increase in capital goods import, gross domestic investments increase by some J\$1.5). The average annual value of gross investments during the period was J\$475 million. One third of this is approximately J\$158 million—that is, virtually the value of the constant term in (6.2) (although the coefficient for the intercept is not significantly different from zero at the five percent test level). The facts that the coefficient for M_c is significantly different from zero at the 5 percent test level (it is, in fact significant even at the 1 percent test level), that the R^2 is relatively high and that there are no signs of auto-correlation (the DW test is inconclusive) suggest that some credibility may be put in the result.

The picture should be rather clear by now. The government's search for revenue has forced it to intensify surplus extraction. The lion's share of this has been appropriated from capitalists. Since the government has also used its surplus income to expand social services, particularly by expanding the public labor force the result is that surplus has been redistributed to a significant degree: labor has gained at capital's expense and middle- and high-income wage recipients have gained at the expense of low-income wage recipients. The result is that the pattern of surplus disposal has changed significantly. Two effects seem to be of some importance. First, since the propensity to save out of surplus income is higher for capitalists than for labor, national savings have fallen at an alarming rate (this effect is enhanced by the fact that the volume of surplus dropped during the better part of the 1970s).[22] Second, the change in the personal distribution of surplus against low-income wage earners has affected the pattern of consumption. Since middle- and high-income wage recipients have a higher propensity to consume imported goods than have low-income wage recipients, the demand for such goods has increased drastically—in particular during the 1970s. Since, during the same decade, exports slumped (largely because of the disappointing performance of the bauxite industry after 1974), the foreign debt grew and the prices of some essential import goods such as oil skyrocketed, the room for importation of non-consumption goods was radically restricted. In particular, imports of capital goods have declined at a rapid rate largely because of lack of foreign exchange. This is all the more serious since Jamaica cannot produce domestic substitutes for imported capital goods. The result is that gross domestic investment has dropped at a rate proportional to the decline of capital goods imports. This has further contributed to economic stagnation.

CONCLUDING REMARKS

Some of the significant changes that have taken place in Jamaica during the past two decades are structural in nature and therefore difficult to correct by means of conventional economic policies. In particular, given the current propensities to save the redistribution of the surplus in favor of middle- and high-income wage recipients seems to present an obstacle to economic growth; yet, it is politically difficult to alter this situation. Insofar as the conclusions of this and the preceding chapter are accepted as basically correct, the major problems of the economy are low savings and a high demand for imported consumption goods. These problems are not idiosyncratic to Jamaica. In a sense, Jamaica during the 1970s, was captured in the same "socialist dilemma" as Chile under Allende.[23] Political promises were being made during the election campaign—promises that could not be fulfilled unless the time perspective was sufficiently long. But impatience is often the hallmark of the electorate, and Jamaica after 1972 proved to be no exception.[24] Huge amounts of resources were transferred from firms to the government and from the government to labor—either in the form of social services or as employment in the public sector. As is often the case when economic realities are ignored, things did not turn out as expected. Even if the Manley government's ambitious social projects had been successful (which they often were not) the situation of the mid-1970s would have been fundamentally unsound. For savings were falling rapidly and importation of consumer goods soared, so eventually problems were bound to emerge: escalating inflation, increasing unemployment, falling productivity, economic stagnation and in its wake, violence—urban riots, increasing criminality and social repression.

With the benefit of hindsight one can note that the PNP government was far too ambitious—at least with regard to time schedules. Yet one must ask why an economy in which more than three quarters of national income constitute surplus repeatedly fails to generate savings sufficient to attain self-sustained growth. This is really the fundamental issue; and there seem to be a shortage of convincing answers. Again, the case of Jamaica seems to have something in common with Chile. Nicholas Kaldor found that excessive consumption constituted the basic problem. The reason for the Chilean stagnation, writes Kaldor (1964, 266-267),

> is to be found in the high propensity to consume of the capitalist class who appear to have spent on personal consumption more than two-thirds of their gross income, or three-quarters of the net income after tax. Though a higher rate of investment is a matter of foreign exchange and not just of savings, it appears from the estimates that as far as savings are concerned the latent resources that could be mobilised through a reduction in luxury consumption would provide adequate resources to raise the rate of capital accumulation in Chile to a level comparable to that of the advanced industrial countries.[25]

Is Kaldor's recipe for Chile in the 1950s also applicable for Jamaica today? Perhaps, but there is one important qualification. Although Kaldor suggests that investable resources may be generated through additional taxes on luxury consumption, an implicit assumption is that the government actually saves and invests a large part of these revenues. In this respect, the lessons of the PNP governments of the 1970s are not comforting. When the Bauxite Levy was introduced in 1974, government revenues increased by approximately 30 percent and government revenues from the mining sector increased from US$270 million during 1964-73 to approximately US$1,690 million during the following decade; yet, as Wesley Hughes (1984) and Omar Davies (1984) point out, only a tiny portion of these essentially "free" resources was actually allocated to expand or improve productive capacity. Although excessive consumption (in particular of imported commodities) certainly has been one of the major problems in Jamaica, intensified surplus appropriation from those that consume imported goods must be combined with a more restrictive behavior of the government with regard to consumption. If capitalists in Jamaica save too little—either because their income is too small or because they prefer an exuberant living—the appropriate role of the government is to use fiscal policies to generate sufficient funds for productive investments.

APPENDIX TO CHAPTER 6:
SURPLUS ACROSS COUNTRIES AND OVER TIME

To check the validity of the results established in Chapters 5 and 6, data has been collected for 23 countries and this Appendix reports on some regression results. The data has, in its entirety, been collected from various issues of the UN's *Yearbook of National Accounts Statistics* and the International Labor Organization's *Yearbook of Labor Statistics*. The results presented here should

Table A6.1
Income and Distribution of Surplus III
in Selected Less-Developed Countries. Annual Averages.

Country	Period	Per Capita Income[a]	Rate of Surplus[b]	Wages	Profits	Taxes
Botswana	1980-83	985	0.86	0.37	0.42	0.21
Cameroon	1980-81	674	0.84	0.26	0.72	0.02
Chile	1980-82	2,575	0.78	0.32	0.52	0.17
Egypt	1977-80	666	0.85	0.30	0.65	0.05
Jamaica	1980-85	2,132	0.81	0.47	0.27	0.26
Kenya	1976-83	419	0.85	0.28	0.64	0.07
South Korea	1980-84	2,067	0.89	0.39	0.51	0.10
Mauritius	1980-84	1,313	0.72	0.23	0.57	0.20
Peru	1980-81	4,747	0.88	0.32	0.56	0.12
Sri Lanka	1983-84	202	0.77	0.27	0.51	0.23
Trinidad	1980-85	5,329	0.79	0.43	0.24	0.33
Venezuela	1980-85	3,660	0.79	0.32	0.42	0.26

Sources: *Yearbook of National Accounts Statistics* (Geneva: United Nations), various issues; *Yearbook of Labor Statistics* (Geneva: International Labor Organization), various issues.

[a] US$, 1980 prices.
[b] Surplus III as share of GDP.

be viewed more as an illustration of how the method of surplus analysis may be applied than an analysis of the mechanisms connecting surplus formation and distribution to economic performance.

The countries are divided into 12 countries with a per capita income of less than US$6,000 in 1980 prices (less developed countries) and 11 with a per capita income exceeding US$6,000. Tables A6.1 and A6.2 provide some basic data. There are significant differences between countries. Thus, for instance, for less-developed countries per capita incomes vary from US$202 (Sri Lanka) to US$5,329 (Trinidad). However, it is notable that although the rate of surplus varies between 72 percent and 89 percent, there does not appear to be any clear correlation between that variable and per capita income. The most distinguishing feature, however, is the distribution of the surplus—in particular that between the private and public shares. The share of net taxes in total Surplus III varies from 2 percent (Cameroon) to 33 percent (Trinidad) so the private share varies significantly. If there are any differences in the way different groups of surplus recipients dispose of their income—in particular, if some groups save and invest a larger fraction of their income than others—the pattern of investment should clearly be reflected in the distribution of the surplus.

Table A6.2
Income and Distribution of Surplus III
in Selected Developed Countries. Annual Averages.

Country	Period	Per Capita Income[a]	Rate of Surplus[b]	Wages	Profits	Taxes
Australia	1980-85	9,837	0.75	0.40	0.28	0.33
Belgium	1980-85	7,581	0.95	0.43	0.38	0.19
Finland	1980-85	7,520	0.78	0.55	0.30	0.15
Germany	1980-84	7,952	0.79	0.54	0.25	0.20
Holland	1980-83	8,171	0.77	0.45	0.29	0.26
Iceland	1980-83	7,331	0.44	0.18	0.26	0.56
Japan	1980-85	6,116	0.81	0.51	0.33	0.16
New Zealand	1980-84	7,998	0.72	0.24	0.38	0.38
Norway	1980-85	11,007	0.80	0.50	0.22	0.28
Sweden	1980-85	11,823	0.72	0.54	0.21	0.25
USA	1980-85	11,157	0.74	0.51	0.23	0.26

Sources: *Yearbook of National Accounts Statistics* (Geneva: United Nations), various issues; *Yearbook of Labor Statistics* (Geneva: International Labor Organization), various issues.
[a] US$, 1980 prices.
[b] Surplus III as share of GDP.

Turning now to developed countries in Table A6.2, the variations among countries are almost as apparent as for less-developed countries. This is what should be expected since any demarcation line between "developed" and "less-developed" countries is bound to be arbitrary. Per capita incomes vary from US$6,116 in Japan to US$11,823 in Sweden and—excluding Iceland—the rate of surplus varies from 72 percent to 95 percent. Iceland is clearly an outlier, both with regard to the rate and distribution of surplus: only 44 percent of GDP is surplus and, of that, 56 percent accrues to the government in the form of net taxes. The explanation is probably that Iceland's economy is based on activities that are classified as agricultural and that most of these activities take place in small enterprises in which profits are not properly distinguished from the wage. For the rest of the countries, the share of the surplus accruing to the government varies significantly: from some 15 percent in Finland to about 38 percent in New Zealand. Again, however, there does not seem to be any significant correlation between the distribution of the surplus and the rate of surplus in GDP. While the Ricardian model as discussed in Chapter 2 does predict a (negative) correlation between income and rate of surplus, it is important to note that this correlation exists because the main activity in the Ricardian model—agricultural—is the subject of diminishing returns. If returns to scale are constant rather than diminishing, the correlation disappears.

CROSS-COUNTRY RESULTS

Using the countries and periods as described in Tables A6.1 and A6.2, some simple tests based on the discussion of classical growth theory as discussed in Chapter 2 are presented next.

First, is there any relation between the rate of surplus and the rate of growth of per capita incomes? Classical theory suggests that the higher the share of surplus in total output, the faster the rate of growth; in classical theory, the rate of surplus determines the growth of per capita incomes, since—with a given pattern of surplus distribution and disposal—the amount of surplus resources that are invested determines the rate of economic growth. Although another plausible hypothesis would be that the rate of growth of per capita income is determined by other factors and that a higher rate of growth determines the rate of surplus since growth is often concentrated to growth poles (see Lewis 1976), establishing correlation, rather than causation, is the primary interest. Regressing the rate of growth of per capita income in constant US$ on the rate of surplus for the 23 countries previously described produces the following result with t-values in parentheses:

$$(A6.1) \quad PC = 0.811 + 0.0479 RS \qquad R^2 = 0.31$$
$$ (43.4) \quad (3.07) \qquad\qquad n = 23.$$

Here, PC is average annual per capita income growth in constant US$, RS is the rate of Surplus III to GDP and n is the number of observations. The coefficient is significant at the 5 percent test level, so this result indicates that there is a positive correlation between the rate of surplus and the growth of income although nothing can be said about the direction of causation.

To pursue the test of classical growth theory further, note that a strategic assumption in that theory is that different groups exhibit different behavior with regard to surplus disposal. In particular, capitalists save and invest a larger fraction of their income than any other group. Hence, if classical growth theory has any relevance, the share of the surplus accruing to capitalists should be positively correlated to the rate of surplus. Using the data set in Tables A6.1 and A6.2 and OLS as the estimation method the result with t-values in parentheses is the following:

$$(A6.2) \quad\qquad PS = -0.013 + 0.599 RS \qquad R^2 = 0.41$$
$$ (-0.12) \quad (3.8) \qquad\qquad n = 23.$$

Here, PS is defined as the share of profits in Surplus III. This result as well supports the classical mechanism of economic growth. Given the definitions of the variables, the insignificance of the intercept is only what would be expected. The important coefficient is that preceding *RS* and it is significant at the 5 percent test level and it indicates that in the data set approximately 60 percent of additional surplus accrues to capitalists (although it should be kept in mind that conventional marginal interpretations are not applicable since cross-sectional, rather than time-series, data are used).

To sum up, the rate of surplus is positively correlated to the rate of growth of per capita incomes and the share of profits in the surplus appears to increase with the surplus. Hence, the share of profits is positively correlated to the rate of growth of per capita incomes—a result that supports the basic classical mechanism of economic growth.

SURPLUS OVER TIME

The data set just discussed cannot be used to examine surplus over time in the individual countries. As shown in Tables A6.1 and A6.2, the periods of time for which data in some countries exist are only a few years. To facilitate a time series analysis, additional data was collected for some of the countries in the data set. The inclusion of countries was based on data availability; countries were chosen for inclusion only when data was available for eight successive years or more. This yields a data set of 14 countries, 7 developed and 7 less developed.

The first thing to check is whether the rate of surplus is related to the level of income. From classical theory, the rate of surplus would be expected to increase with income—at least as long as the growth of the labor supply in the agricultural sector does not fall short of the rate of growth labor demand outside that sector; that is, as long as the subsistence wage does not increase. If the economy is not characterized by surplus labor, however, economic growth may be expected to crease temporary shortages of labor and consequently a rise in the agricultural wage rate. In this case the rate of surplus is expected to be negatively correlated to the level of income.

Table A6.3 presents the results of the regressions of rate of Surplus III in GDP (*RS*) on the level of per capita income, measured in 1980 US$ (*PCY*). A quick glance reveals that there appears to be no significant correlation between these variables in seven of the countries: Australia, Botswana, Finland, Jamaica, Kenya, Korea and Venezuela. In all these, the *t*-values are not significant at the 5 percent test level and in five of the cases the R^2 is less than 0.1. In the remaining seven countries, however, the R^2 varies between 0.24 (Sweden) and 0.84 (Mauritius) and the coefficients are significant at the 5 percent test level. These countries include both developed and less-developed countries and it is noteworthy that the rate of surplus is negatively related to the level of per capita income in all of them. This suggests that an increase in the level of income is associated with a fall in the rate of surplus, or, more

Table A6.3

Regressions of Rate of Surplus on Real Per Capita Income (*PCY*). Individual Countries.

Country	Period	Intercept	*PCY*	R^2
Australia[a]	1970-85	0.71*	3.9	0.03
Botswana[a]	1972-80	0.89*	—31.8	0.05
Finland	1970-85	0.87*	—12.1	0.13
Holland[a]	1970-83	0.83*	—6.6*	0.57
Jamaica[a]	1970-85	0.82*	—1.3	0.05
Japan[a]	1970-85	0.89*	—10.2*	0.28
Kenya	1972-80	0.84*	21.0	0.01
Korea[a]	1971-84	0.75*	71.0	0.03
Mauritius[a]	1976-84	0.77*	—38.9*	0.84
New Zealand	1981-84	0.76*	—5.0*	0.30
Peru[a]	1972-81	0.89*	—3.5*	0.67
Sweden[a]	1970-85	0.75*	—3.0*	0.24
USA	1970-85	0.94*	—18.2*	0.76
Venezuela[a]	1975-85	0.75*	10.7	0.28

Sources: *Yearbook of National Accounts Statistics* (New York: UN), various issues; *Yearbook of Labor Statistics* (Geneva: ILO), various issues.

[a] Equation corrected for autocorrelation using the Cochrane-Orcutt procedure.

* Coefficient significantly different from zero at the 5 percent test level.

specifically, that income growth in these countries seems to have taken place primarily in the subsistence sector; the average agricultural wage has risen faster that average income. This means that mechanism of growth in the sense of Chapter 2, that is, that non-agricultural sectors grow by tapping resources from the agricultural sector, does not hold water. To the contrary, the results in the table suggest that these countries are not characterized by surplus labor in the agricultural sector.

Finally, the hypothesis discussed in Chapter 6 is examined, that is, that the distribution as well as the size of the surplus determines the rate of private savings. To do that, an equation similar to (6.1) is formulated with the provisos that data are not logged here and the rate of private savings (SH_{pr}) is related to the size of the surplus (measured as Surplus III in 1980 US$; *S3*) and to *I*, the share of profits in the private surplus (see note 11 in Chapter 6 for a definition of this variable). The results are presented in Table A6.4.

In 9 of the 14 equations, the variable *I* is significantly related to the rate of private savings at the 5 percent test level and *S3* is significant in 6 equations. Although it would be rash to draw any definitive conclusions based on these regressions, the results in Table A6.4 at the very least suggest that analysis of the size and distribution of the surplus along the lines discussed in Chapter 6 may prove instructive for an understanding of the process of economic growth

Table A6.4
Regressions of Rate of Private Savings on Distribution of Private Surplus (*I*)
and Surplus III (*S3*). Individual Countries.

Country	Period	Intercept	I	S3	R^2
Australia[a]	1970-85	0.05	0.79	—0.07	0.62
Botswana[a]	1972-80	0.08	0.402	—0.08	0.10
Finland[a]	1970-85	—0.15	0.58	0.35*	0.66
Holland[a]	1970-83	—1.12*	0.52*	1.56*	0.95
Jamaica[a]	1970-85	0.2	0.72	—0.37	0.26
Japan	1970-85	0.19*	0.44*	—0.02	0.87
Kenya[a]	1972-80	—1.02	0.38	1.12	0.22
Korea[a]	1971-84	0.64*	—0.42*	—0.19	0.34
Mauritius[a]	1976-84	0.13	0.89	—0.64	0.13
NewZealand	1981-84	—0.68*	0.43*	1.03*	0.66
Peru[a]	1972-81	—1.95*	0.56*	2.14*	0.56
Sweden[a]	1970-85	0.62*	0.83*	—0.83	0.54
USA[a]	1970-85	—0.83*	1.11*	0.97*	0.69
Venezuela	1975-85	—2.25*	—0.37	3.11*	0.89

Sources: *Yearbook of National Accounts Statistics* (New York: UN), various issues;
Yearbook of Labor Statistics (Geneva: ILO), various issues.
[a] Equation corrected for autocorrelation using the Cochrane-Orcutt procedure.
* Coefficient significantly different from zero at the 5 percent test level.

and distribution. In particular, the tentative results presented in this Appendix suggest that the economic growth at the aggregate level takes place much according to Classical rules.

NOTES

1. Some indications of this can be found in Tables 5.2 and 5.6. However, the data here are aggregated so it is impossible to follow yearly changes. Danielson (1990, Tables 1 and 2) provides more details to support the arguments made in the text.

2. Figures are taken from the national accounts except for the GDP deflator that comes from IMF (1988). Data concerning Jamaica's modern macroeconomic history can be found in Danielson (1993, Ch. 3).

3. Of the five major studies of Manley's Jamaica appearing during the last ten years or so (Kaufman 1985; Stephens and Stephens 1986; Gayle 1986, Chs. 1-2, 5-6; Hope 1987; Boyd 1988) all deal extensively with fiscal policy and—save for Boyd (1988) who concentrates on poverty issues—with the bauxite levy. None of these authors, however, examine the consequences of the PNP's search for revenue and there are also not many studies dealing with the long-term consequences of the changed patters of public spending. Girvan et al. (1980, 199) suggest that the first PNP government was

"tilting the balance between the public and private sector, and between labour and capital." This point, however, is not pursued further.

4. All figures presented in this paragraph have been collected from IMF (1988, 440-441). Danielson (1993, Ch. 6) provides further details.

5. Stephens and Stephens (1986, 69-81) provide a description of some of these projects as do Girvan et al. (1980, 116-118).

6. Hughes (1984, 68). Whether the implementation of the levy actually caused the decline of the mining sector is still a debated issue. Stephens and Stephens (1985; 1986, 129) hold the view that the decline of the mining operations in Jamaica was planned by the mining corporations long before the implementation of the levy. See also the various papers in JBI (1984).

7. Girvan et al. (1980, 142) notes with regard to fiscal performance: "Personal income taxes proved to be the most buoyant of the tax categories, because of the substantial increases in money wages, but corporate tax payments were virtually stagnant and actually declined in 1974/75. The government introduced additional indirect taxation, especially consumption duties, and resorted to increasing transfers from the Capital Development Fund into which the production Levy was paid."

8. Jamaica's international credit rating dropped from A to D; Girvan et al. (1980, 118).

9. Calculations based on material included in the sources quoted in the Appendix to Chapter 5.

10. First-rate introductions to the post-Keynesian literature include Kregel (1975) and Sawyer (1982, esp. Ch. 5). Note, however, that this assumption was standard in classical economics, vanishing only as marginalist theories emphasizing individual rational choice gained dominance.

11. This index of surplus distribution is defined as

$$(n6.1) \qquad\qquad I = \frac{\Pi^D}{\Pi^D + e^D L},$$

where, as before, Π is profits, e is "excess" wage rate and L is employment. Superscript D stands for disposable, that is, net of income taxes.

12. Since private savings were negative in 1976, this year has been treated as a missing value.

13. The data sources are reported in the Appendix to Chapter 5.

14. See, for instance, Mikesell and Zinser (1973), Snyder (1974) or Gersowitz (1988, Sec. 3).

15. The critical value for the F-test at the 5 percent significance level is 3.16 with 3 and 20 degrees of freedom, respectively.

16. None of the coefficients is however significantly larger than unity at the five percent test level.

17. In defence of classical economics, however, it should be recorded that if it is assumed that those who save also are the ones that invest, the need for a capital market disappears and savings will, at least in the absence of international trade, by definition

equal investments and indeed automatically will be translated into investment. In much of classical thought, this is precisely the assumption made. However, in the era after Keynes it is difficult to find any excuse for making such an assumption since the failure of savings to reach investors may be one of the causes of stagnation.

18. Calculated from NIP (1981, 1984).

19. Although agriculture is outstanding as a low income sector, the trend in distribution during the 1970s was similar. Thus for instance, the data in the national accounts (NIP 1981, 1984) show that while approximately half of the employed labor force in the early 1970s worked in these two sectors, only some 20 percent of total wages accrued to them.

20. Danielson (1986, Table 2.2) calculates that the economy-wide wage increased from being approximately 5.5 times higher than the agricultural wage in 1972 to being approximately 8.4 times higher in 1984.

21. Data comes from IMF (1988) and from *External Trade*, various issues.

22. Although the *share* of surplus in GDP increased, the *volume* of surplus fell. These two are compatible, of course, only because GDP fell as well.

23. However, whether the international opposition was the same in Manley's Jamaica as in Allende's Chile is a disputed issue. Manley (1982, 223-237) has no doubts that American interests (in particular the Central Intelligence Agency) supported and partly financed local groups antagonistic to the PNP. de Vylder (1974) and Nove (1976) provide excellent analyses of the *Unidad Popular's* economic policies.

24. Details concerning opportunism and clientelism in Jamaican politics are provided in Danielson and Lundahl (1992).

25. Kaldor's work in Chile is evaluated by Palma and Marcel (1989). It should be noted that Kaldor's usage of "capitalist" differs from that adopted here. Since the first Chilean national accounts publications after the Second World War contained enormous amounts of data regarding the distribution of rents and the personal distribution of income, Kaldor was able to trace the disposal of property income accruing to individuals (the publication of such information was soon to be discontinued, partly as a result of Kaldor's analysis). Jamaican national accounts contain no such information.

7

The Role of Interest Groups

Chapters 5 and 6 have analyzed the basic reasons for stagnation in Jamaica. Recall from Chapter 2 that the classical mechanism of economic growth may be formulated as consisting of two stages—the size of the surplus and how the surplus is disposed of—it seems that in a Jamaican context, the first stage does not present a problem. The surplus as it has been calculated in these chapters constitutes by far the largest component of total production—so large, in fact, that any reasonable definition of "subsistence" would imply a surplus of more than half of net domestic product.[1] The uses to which surplus resources have been put, on the other hand, seem to be the basic obstacle for economic growth. As seen in Chapter 5, only a small amount of the surplus is saved and invested; hence, most of it is consumed. The material presented in Chapter 6 suggests an important conclusion, namely that the deteriorating private savings behavior observed in the 1970s was caused by a change in the government's fiscal policies, the link between government policies and private savings being changes in the functional distribution of surplus income. Insofar as this is a valid interpretation of events, it may be suggested that the government's behavior is important, not to say crucial, for the performance of the economy. Although this is not a very original suggestion in general, it deserves to be emphasized in a study of the Jamaican economy since, as noted in previous chapters, several writers—for example, Girvan et al. (1980)—attribute the causes of the stagnation to external factors, in particular the IMF.

From the observation that the government plays an important part in shaping an economy's destiny, the suggestion that the government may act to achieve particular goals for particular groups is not far away. Development economists have relatively recently incorporated such considerations in their models.[2] The basic idea is very simple. In a democratic country, the government is elected by the public. Assuming that voters are rational and interested in their own welfare, the outcome of the election will be determined by two factors. First are the promises made by the different parties during the campaign, that is, a rational individual cast his vote in favor of the party that he believes best serves his interests. From this angle, the election campaign may be seen as an advertising process in which parties try to win voters. Second is the relative credibility of the parties.[3] This means that rational voters judge parties not only with respect to campaign promises but also with respect to how well promises have been fulfilled in the past. The credibility issue is important, since it implies that parties have an incentive to let the public think that promises are always fulfilled. If the party relies on particular groups for basic support, the party, if elected, will probably favor these groups by offering them public jobs, protection from imports and the like.[4] This means that the elected party also has an incentive to hide that particular groups are favored if additional votes are required to win the election. In the terminology of Magee et al. (1989), the government has an incentive to obfuscate.

This chapter asks whether the available data favor the hypothesis of a non-neutral government. The answer is the affirmative; the evidence suggests not only that Jamaican governments consistently have favored some groups and sectors at the expense of others, but also that the basic reasons for doing so have been political, that is, the governments have acted to increase the probability of winning the next election. The analysis is framed within the theory of sectoral clashes and coalitions, developed by Markos Mamalakis (1969, 1971). This theory emphasizes that governments often form coalitions with particular groups in society and that such favorization may lead to "clashes" in the economy—conflicts that not necessarily put different classes on opposite sides but that instead may lead to intersectoral "struggles for the surplus." Due to nonavailability of sectoral labor data, the analysis is limited to the period 1970-84.

THE SECTORAL DISTRIBUTION OF THE SURPLUS

First, the sectoral distribution of the surplus, as defined in Chapter 3, is analyzed. Using the notation as presented in that chapter, the surplus in sector j is defined as

(7.1) $S^j = Y^j - \delta K^j - sL^j = e^D L^j + \Pi^{D,j} + T_d^j + T_i^j - Z^j$.

This is the general formulation of the surplus. However, since data on the sectoral distribution of income tax revenue is not readily available a more useful form is Surplus I which, for sector j, is given by

(7.2) $S_I^j = Y^j - \delta K^j - sL^j = eL^j + \Pi^j + T_i^j - Z^j$.

In principle, however, it is possible to calculate both S_{II}^j and S_{III}^j ,given that sufficiently detailed information concerning tax laws and practice are available. However, since income tax concessions are not likely to be given on a sectoral basis, the rate and pattern of income taxation is likely to be similar throughout sectors that implies that (7.2) gives a fairly accurate picture of the sectoral distribution of surplus.

Before the calculations are presented and analyzed, a word of method is warranted. The Jamaican national accounts use a slightly different sectoral classification from the Jamaican labor statistics. To be able to use these two sources in the same study some aggregation has to be carried out. Later, an explanation of how this aggregation has been made is provided. Further, following Mamalakis (1969), the important distinction between goods which are potential export goods and other goods is introduced. Since Jamaica does not possess any capital goods industries, export industries are necessary to earn foreign exchange. In this sense, the export sector becomes a quasi-capital goods sector.

The Classification of Sectors

The classification of sectors can be made on two basic grounds—statistical and economic. Some use of both shall be made. First is the statistical classification. This follows essentially the classification in the national

Table 7.1
Sectoral Distribution of Output (Y) and Employment (L).
Statistical Classification. Jamaica, 1970-84. Percent.

	1970-74		1975-79		1980-84	
	Y	L	Y	L	Y	L
Agriculture	7.0	29.7	8.0	35.2	6.7	34.4
Manufacturing	16.2	12.6	16.8	10.7	16.9	12.0
Mining	9.7	1.0	10.8	1.0	8.3	1.1
Construction	10.9	7.9	7.3	5.0	7.4	3.7
Services	56.2	48.8	57.1	48.1	60.7	48.8
of which						
Government	9.4	11.0	13.2	15.5	13.5	14.4
Distribution	19.2	13.1	16.4	12.5	19.5	14.0
Other	27.6	24.7	27.5	20.1	27.7	20.4

Sources: Labor data: AAS (1971, Table 17); RLF (1980, 3-4); RLF (1984, 2-4). National accounts data: NIP (1981, Table 6); NIP (1984, Table 7).

accounts with the reservation that some sectors have been aggregated into "Other Services." The sectors used are: Agriculture, Manufacturing, Mining, Construction and Services. Services, in turn, are divided into Government, Distribution and Other Services. The last item includes—in terms of the national accounts—Electricity and Water; Transport, Storage, and Communication; Financing and Insurance; Real Estate and Business Services; and Miscellaneous Services. Admittedly, it would be interesting to study the development of the surplus in such sectors as, for example, Financing and Insurance. However, the available labor market data does not allow this. In Table 7.1, the distribution of output and labor for these sectors are depicted.

Second is the economic classification. The basic idea here is to aggregate sectors that produce commodities with essentially the same economic characteristics. In particular, it is important to distinguish, first, between consumer goods and capital goods and, second, between consumer goods and services. Services are, of course, produced in the service sectors; in the classification here, these consist of Government, Distribution and Other Services. Capital goods are intermediary goods used, directly or indirectly, in the production of other goods. As noted above, since Jamaica has no capital goods industries, the value of output in the mining sector is taken to represent the potential for importation of capital goods; the mining sector becomes, in Mamalakis' words, a "quasi-capital goods industry."[5] Furthermore, the construction sector, the output of which consists essentially of buildings and other infra structure, can be interpreted as producing capital goods. Table 7.2 depicts sectoral output and employment in Jamaica according to this classification.

It is clear from Table 7.2 that the quasi-capital goods sectors have contracted considerably during the period—both in terms of output and employment. It is noteworthy that the consumption goods industries have expanded their share of employment, while the service industries have increased their share of output. From Table 7.1 it might be inferred that it is Agriculture in which the employment expansion has been most significant,

Table 7.2
Sectoral Distribution of Output (Y) and Employment (L).
Economic Classification. Jamaica, 1970-84. Percent.

	1970-74		1975-79		1980-84	
	Y	L	Y	L	Y	L
Consumption Goods	23.2	42.3	24.8	45.9	23.6	46.4
Capital Goods	20.6	8.9	18.1	6.0	15.7	4.8
Services	56.2	48.8	57.1	48.1	60.7	48.8

Source: Labor data: AAS (1971, Table 17); RLF (1980, 3-4); RLF (1984, 2-4). National accounts data: NIP (1981, Table 6); NIP (1984, Table 7).

whereas manufacturing output has remained approximately constant, and that the lion's part of the output expansion of Services has taken place in the government sector. Employment in the government sector has not increased in proportion to value of output. Since approximately 90 percent of production costs in that sector is cost of labor, it can be inferred that the average wage cost in that sector has increased over the period.

Distribution of the Surplus

Turning now to the surplus and its distribution, Table 7.3 depicts the sectoral distribution of the surplus as defined by (7.2). As can be seen from that table, the sectoral distribution of the surplus resembles the sectoral distribution of GDP. Although the shares of surplus and GDP, respectively, accruing to each sector are not equal, the pattern of change is almost the same. Thus for instance the share of surplus and GDP accruing to Agriculture declines consistently, whereas the share accruing, for example, to Government increases.

It can also be seen from Table 7.3 that the distribution of the surplus between the economically defined sectors changes drastically. Although the share accruing to consumption goods sectors (Agriculture and Manufacturing) remains virtually constant (it increases from 21.8 percent in 1970-74 to 23.5 percent in 1975-79 and decreases to 21.8 percent in 1980-84), the share accruing to quasi-capital goods sectors falls from 20.8 percent in 1970-74 to 19.4 percent in 1975-79 and finally to 16.6 percent of total surplus in 1980-84. This fall in surplus has occurred in favor of the service sector, which has expanded during the period from 57 percent to almost 62 percent of total surplus. In particular, it is Government and Other Services that account for the

Table 7.3
Sectoral Distribution of the Surplus.
Jamaica, 1970-84. Percent. Annual Averages.

	1970/74	1975/79	1980/84
Agriculture	5.0	5.3	3.8
Manufacture	16.9	18.2	18.0
Mining	9.0	11.7	8.5
Construction	11.8	7.7	8.1
Services	57.3	57.1	61.6
of which			
(Government)	(10.3)	(14.6)	(14.9)
(Distribution)	(20.7)	(16.0)	(16.8)
(Other)	(26.3)	(26.5)	(29.9)

Sources: Labor data: AAS (1971, Table 17); RLF (1980, 3-4); RLF (1984, 2-4). National accounts data: NIP (1981, Table 6); NIP (1984, Table 7).

lion's part of the increase; the share of surplus accruing to Distribution's does in fact decline.

Turning now to the functional distribution of the surplus, Table 7.4 depicts the share of the sectoral surplus accruing to private actors—that is, as profits ("Operating Surplus") and "excess" wages. Recall from Chapter 3 that agricultural labor does not receive any surplus. The private share of the surplus in that sector thus accrues as profits.

On average, about 90 percent of the surplus accrues—gross of income taxes—to private actors. This share, however, varies widely between sectors. Although, for instance, in Construction and Government almost the entire surplus accrues to private actors, about 30 percent of the surplus in Manufacturing is extracted in the form of indirect taxes. Note also the extremely low share accruing to private actors in the Mining sector—in particular during the two latter subperiods. This is entirely due to the implementation of the Bauxite Levy in 1974: a tax on mining output, linked to the world market price of aluminium.[6]

Noteworthy is also the development of the private share in Distribution. It increases from less than 82 percent in 1970-74 to over 95 percent in 1975-79. This feature might—at least in part—be explained by the erratic movements of subsidies to that sector.[7]

One possible suggestion from Table 7.4 is thus that the government does not tax the different sectors equally. Ignoring the special treatment of the mining sector, the fact still remains that although some sectors are subject to negligible indirect tax rates, in other sectors more that 30 percent of the total surplus generated is extracted as net indirect taxes.

The fact that Manufacturing is the subject of the highest net indirect tax

Table 7.4
Private Share of Sectoral Surplus.
Jamaica, 1970-84. Percent. Annual Averages.

	1970/74	1975/79	1980/84
Agriculture	100.2	99.8	97.1
Manufacture	71.8	64.3	66.5
Mining[a]	70.7	34.9	37.7
Construction	100.0	100.0	99.9
Services	90.5	95.0	92.0
of which			
(Government)	(100.0)	(99.9)	(99.8)
(Distribution)	(81.6)	(95.1)	(90.2)
(Others)	(94.6)	(92.3)	(93.5)
Total	**89.7**	**90.2**	**89.0**

Sources: Labor data: AAS (1971, Table 17); RLF (1980, 3-4); RLF (1984, 2-4). National accounts data: NIP (1981, Table 6); NIP (1984, Table 7).
[a] Net of bauxite levy

rates leaves the impression of outright discrimination. Because Manufacturing receives a relatively large and increasing volume of subsidies.[8] This policy, of course, is part of the general incentives program, designed to stimulate investment in and expansion of the manufacturing sector.[9] Since the major part of the incentives legislation is specifically directed toward specific manufacturing subsectors (in particular, foreign firms and firms producing for export), it seems as if the manufacturing subsectors that do not fulfill the requirements of the incentives legislation are exposed to a—relatively speaking—very high rate of indirect taxation.

Finally, looking at the distribution of the surplus for the economically defined sectors,[10] the share accruing to private actors declines in consumption as well as in quasi-capital goods sectors. In the former, the private share declines from over 80 percent in 1970-74 to a little more than 75 percent a decade later. In the quasi-capital goods sectors, the private share declines from about 86 percent in 1970-74 to a little over 60 percent in 1975-79. Much of this decline is due to the implementation of the bauxite levy. However, in 1980-84, the private share recovers somewhat, reaching 67 percent of total surplus in the quasi-capital sectors. As can be immediately seen from the table, the share of the surplus in the service sectors accruing to private actors increases by a few percentage points during the first half of the period and declines somewhat during the latter.

The distribution of the private share of the surplus is indicated in Table 7.5 which depicts the share of the sectoral surplus accruing to labor. Recall from Chapter 3 that since "subsistence" is defined as the average agricultural wage, labor in the agricultural sector does not receive any surplus. Recall also that profits by definition do not show up in the government sector; labor's share of the surplus in that sector is thus equal to the private share of the surplus.

Table 7.5
Labor's Share of the Surplus.
Jamaica, 1970-84. Percent. Annual Averages.

	1970/74	1975/79	1980/84
Manufacture	41.3	46.2	41.6
Mining	35.1	24.3	35.1
Construction	86.7	90.2	80.2
Services	54.1	61.6	56.0
of which			
(Government)	(100.0)	(99.9)	(99.5)
(Distribution)	(39.2)	(35.2)	(26.5)
(Others)	(48.1)	(58.2)	(55.7)
Total	**51.1**	**53.2**	**50.6**

Sources: Labor data: AAS (1971, Table 17); RLF (1980, 3-4); RLF (1984, 2-4). National accounts data: NIP (1981, Table 6); NIP (1984, Table 7).

On average, labor receives about half of the total surplus in the form of "excess" wages. The table shows that it is two sectors—Services and Construction—in which labor's share exceeds the economy-wide average, and in one of these—Services—this is very much due to the definition of output in the government sector.

Note that labor's share of the surplus in Mining declines significantly during the first half of the period. This is the approximate pattern found for the private share. This suggests that although profits suffer from the bauxite levy, capitalists do not carry the entire burden of that tax: wages also decline in relation to average labor productivity. This is worth noting, because the intention of the tax was to ensure that stop the outflow of invisible profits.

In some other sectors, the variations in labor's share do not follow the variations in the private share. In Manufacturing, labor's share increases when the private share decreases and decreases when the private share increases. This implies that the share of profits in Manufacturing's surplus varies considerably: from over 30 percent in 1970-74 to about 18 percent in 1975-79 and about 25 percent in 1980-84.

Similarly, Table 7.4 showed that the private share of the surplus in Distribution increased by some 13 percentage points during the first half of the period. Labor's share declines during the same time by about 4 percentage units, implying that between 1970-74 and 1975-79 the share of profits in the distribution sector's surplus increase from a little more than 40 percent to almost 60 percent of total sectoral surplus.

Note also the sharp fall of surplus accruing to labor in Construction in the latter half of the period: from 90 to 80 percent. Since the private share of the surplus remains virtually constant, this implies that the share of profits doubles during this time: from 10 to 20 percent of the surplus.

The distribution of the surplushas been examined, both between sectors and between income groups within sectors. The principal findings are that the surplus is unequally distributed between sectors; that the distribution of the surplus between private and public surplus recipients differs between sectors with relatively large variations; and that the distribution of the private surplus between "excess" wages and profits varies depending on the sector. These findings constitute the basis from which a number of implications shall be discussed. Specifically, the fact that the surplus is unequally distributed in sectors suggests that economic agents can find it profitable to engage in a "struggle for the surplus" along the lines sketched by Markos Mamalakis' (1969, 1971) theory of sectoral clashes and coalitions. It is argued here that Mamalakis' theory provides a fruitful starting point for a discussion of the role of the state in Jamaica (or, for that matter, in many democratic or semi-democratic developing countries). Before turning to that theory, however, it may prove fruitful to discuss in some detail the evidence for a non-neutral government in Jamaica.

THE ECONOMICS OF POLITICS IN JAMAICA

Jamaica attained internal self-government in 1959 and political independence in 1962. Two political parties dominate the stage: The Jamaican Labour Party (JLP) and the People's National Party (PNP). Since 1959, eight general elections have been held with the PNP winning four times (1959, 1972, 1976 and 1990) and the JLP as well winning four times (1962, 1967, 1980 and 1983). Although both parties have grown out of the trade union movements in the 1930s, the JLP is often marked as being more "conservative" and the PNP is characterized as "democratic socialist." The PNP have since the 1960s advocated policies limiting the effects of "market forces"; consequently, import substitution and public participation in economic life have been issues high on that party's agenda. The political platform of the JLP has changed markedly between the 1960s and the 1980s. Although the party has paid lip service to free markets and deregulation, the actual policies pursued in the 1960s—in particular under Prime Ministers Donald Sangster and Hugh Lawson Shearer—emphasized the importance of industrialization behind tariff barriers and led to a relatively rapid expansion of public activities in the economic life. However, the JLP of the 1980s—led by Edward Seaga—pursued a relatively consistent policy of deregulation and reduction of public participation in the economic sphere (Stephens & Stephens 1986, Ch. 7).

Using the right-left scale as a rough measurement of party platforms, it seems likely that the more conservative JLP finds support among capitalists and high-income professionals, whereas the PNP relies relatively more heavily on backing from small farmers, peasant workers and blue collar labor (Stone 1981). Furthermore, since the JLP (at least during the 1980s) advocated more market oriented policies, a large share of the Jamaican business community would be expected to support that party.

A brief comparison of the policies pursued by the two parties basically confirms this view. From Carl Stone's (1988, Table 22) listing of the most important policies implemented by the PNP in 1972-80 and the JLP in 1980-87, it may be concluded that four out of seven PNP policy measures had small farmers, workers, trade unions and students as their major beneficiaries whereas four out of eight JLP policy measures benefited primarily investors, importers, merchants and hoteliers.

However, Jamaica is a country with little class-based voting; both parties have to earn their votes. This implies that the voting pattern will be rather sensitive to how actual policies are perceived by voters. Thus for instance, although the majority of the business and management class and the high-income professionals voted for the PNP in 1972, only a minor fraction did so in 1976 and 1980. Similarly, a majority of the manual wage laborers voted for the PNP in 1972, a majority that increased in 1976 and fell drastically in the 1980 elections (Stone, 1980, 37).

In such an economy, it most likely that policies are formed endogenously, that is, that interest groups succeed in influencing the formation of policies. Consequently, the channels through which influence can be forwarded and the efficiency with which that influence can be exerted will be strategic to the outcome of the election.

The Objectives

The PNP and the JLP have used, to a varying extent, three basic methods of securing votes: they have tried to distinguish themselves from the competing party in order to secure a broad base of "safe" votes; they have resorted to patronage; and they have been willing to obey lobbies to secure additional economic and political support. Each one of these methods will be dealt with in turn.

Although the actual policies pursued by the JLP during the 1960s did not differ very much from the policies pursued by the PNP during the 1970s, party platforms have always emphasized different issues. The PNP platform stresses the importance of an equal distribution of income and rapid eradication of poverty, whereas the JLP focuses on production and the benefits of the market. Due to this emphasis of the socialist (or anti-socialist) ideology of the party, some voters may be less willing to give up their support even if the actual policies pursued is not entirely in line with this platform. However, the vote-maximizing strategy in a two-party framework is to pursue policies that are rather similar to those of the competing party. The balance between pursuing "platform policies" (in order to keep the safe voters) and pursuing policies that attract marginal voters is a delicate one, for the ruling party must be able to (a) show evidence of platform loyalty and (b) attract a sufficient number of marginal voters in order to be reelected.[11]

The JLP of the 1980s, however, was a party that differed substantially from the JLP of the 1960s. Party Leader and Prime Minister (as well as Minister of Finance and Minister of Defense and Communication) Edward Seaga stressed the ideological differences between the JLP and the PNP and attempted to implement policies consistent with the JLP platform in practice. In particular, the JLP of the 1980s emphasized the role of the market and the importance of giving production high priority. This stands in sharp contrast to the PNP policies of the 1970s, which gave precedence to issues of income distribution. In terms of politically favored groups, this indicates that the JLP favors private sector producers over labor. Table 7.6 shows some indicators of how certain policies have changed from the PNP period of the 1970s to the JLP period of the 1980s. It is rather clear that the JLP (i) turned the functional distribution of income in favor of capital; (ii) increased gross profits in relation to food consumption; (iii) diminished tax rates on income and profit at the expense of

Table 7.6
Indicators of Policy Change Between the PNP and the JLP.

	PNP	JLP
Profits/Wages (%)	31[a]	51[d]
Profits/Food purchased (%)	117[a]	130[d]
Distribution of Tax burden		
(% of total taxes)		
Corporate	19[b]	14[d]
Indirect	38[b]	59[d]
Household income	23[b]	27[d]
Subsidies to households and firms	106[c]	11[d]
(millions J$, 1974 prices)		

Source: Stone (1988, Table 16).
[a] 1975 [b] 1980 [c] 1978 [d] 1985

indirect taxes and consequently levied a higher tax burden on low-income earners; and (iv) drastically cut government subsidies to households and firms, implying in particular a reduction in the standard of living of the poor (Stone, 1988). It would appear that the JLP policies have favored producers over consumers and capital over labor. In the light of the previous discussion, this can be interpreted as an attempt to emphasize the ideological differences between the parties and to establish a firm basis of safe voters.

The second method used to secure additional votes has been the use of patronage. Through government contracts, public employment, direct handouts of money, housing and services, party members have been rewarded for backing the ruling party. During the JLP government of the 1960s it was almost impossible to get a government sponsored job or contract without JLP membership (Kaufman 1985, 52). The Tivoli Gardens project is probably one of the more flagrant examples of patronage. The Tivoli Gardens, a PNP-dominated shantytown in downtown Kingston, became the subject of urban renewal in the early 1960s. The JLP government sent bulldozers, police and army in, cleared the area of PNP supporters and renovated the entire shantytown. Thereafter, flats were allocated to JLP members, possibly as a compensation for hard and loyal party work. Incidentally, the Tivoli Gardens is part of the constituency of Edward Seaga, then minister of development and welfare, later prime minister (Kaufman 1985, 113).[12]

Further, ardent PNP supporters were frequently rewarded with government sponsored jobs during the 1970s. This form of vote seeking was complemented with the (unofficial) support of youth gangs which in exchange for handouts and short-term employment helped preserve party territory—sometimes with knives and rocks, sometimes with M16's. The escalating violence surrounding Jamaican elections may to a large extent be attributed to the actions of such gangs (see Kaufman 1985, 112-115; Lacey 1977).

In a small economy—Jamaica has some 2 million inhabitants—issues and policies easily become personalized. Hence, not only groups and organizations but individuals as well may be able to influence the direction of policy. In Jamaica, three families have been particularly influential without actually participating in politics: the Matalon family, associated to the PNP and the Ashenheim and the Henriques families associated to the JLP (Stone 1988). In the survey conducted by Evelyne and John Stephens (1986, Appendices 2 and 4), members of these families are ranked as being among the most influential individuals outside politics throughout the 1970s and during the first years of the 1980s. Reid (1977) demonstrates clearly how, in 1975, the 21 dominating families—with the Ashenheim, Henriques and Matalon families at the top— were linked to each other in five "supergroups" and accounted for 125 of 219 directorships and nearly 70 percent of all company chairmanships.

But interest groups have formed strong lobbies as well. As noted, both parties have a strong trade union backing, through which blue- and white-collar labor channel their policy pressures. Trade unions are also a major source of finance for political campaigns. As for producers, strong lobby groups exist, representing the Jamaica Chamber of Commerce, the Jamaica Manufacturers Association, the Jamaica Hotel and Tourist Organization, the Sugar Manufactures Organization and so on. Most of these interest groups are also organized in the Private Sector of Jamaica (PSoJ), an umbrella organization representing all private business regardless of sector.

Given that the JLP stresses production and the market relatively more than the PNP, it is not very surprising that producers' lobbying groups (in particular the Chamber of Commerce) have openly supported the JLP. By an appropriate combination of policies after the takeover in 1980, the JLP government could change the tax and expenditure strategy in favor of those groups that would give large economic support to the party (cf. Table 7.6). Thus, for instance, by combining import deregulation with an abandonment of the PNP-implemented policy of free tuition to university students, producers could be favored without too much strain being put on the budget.

Lobbying is not a new phenomenon in Jamaica. Discussing the political situation around independence, Rex Nettleford (1971, xxiv-xxv) notes that "the leaders were indistinguishable in terms of background or ideological commitment; the financing of both parties became dependent on entrepreneurial beneficence rather than solely on grass-root and members' contribution and policies as implemented bore marked similarities."

However, it seems as if the role of lobbies has grown in importance during the 1980s, that lobbies have been increasingly cogent in influencing policy formation. According to Carl Stone (1988, 70):

Some key members of the private sector hold important government jobs and control important ministries as well as provide important policy leadership roles for the JLP government. . . . Several very influential business personalities maintain close contact with the Prime Minister. . . . Some serve as key advisors behind the scenes. Private sector influence over policy making has therefore considerably increased since 1980, although access to power has been limited to the big business families, foreign business interests and interests that have given generously to the JLP campaign financing.

The lobbies respond to unfavorable policies by cutting their financial support rather than publicly criticizing government action (Stone, 1988, 63-64):

The leaderships of these private sector lobbies seek more often to be supportive of government policies rather than to criticise. They fear the power of big government and the reprisals that could come from political leaders who view their criticism as political attacks. They make public criticisms of government policies only in extreme situations where they feel that vital private sector interests are being threatened and they do so only as a last resort after other channels of response are fully exhausted.

By way of summary, there are three basic ways of gaining votes and establishing a firm basis of political support in Jamaican politics. First, the party may use rhetoric in order to distinguish itself from the competing party and thereby forming a large cadre of safe voters. Second, the party may reward loyal party members in the form of housing, services, employment or direct, pecuniary benefits. Associated to this patronage is the clandestine support of youth gangs that help to protect party territory (see Chevannes 1981 for a fascinating story of the formation of youth gangs in Kingston). Finally, the party may accept pressure from interest groups, that is, the ruling party may be willing to implement certain policies in return for economic and political support. As far as Jamaica is concerned, it seems quite clear both that lobbying is a time-honored activity and that it has become more important as the JLP regained power in 1980. As shall be seen later, the two parties have relied on somewhat dissimilar methods of attracting voters and, moreover, these methods seem to have changed over time. All these methods, however, seem to have one thing in common: they are designed to obfuscate, to increase the costs to opponents and voters of revealing the government's true intent.

The Methods

The government chooses to support certain groups. This also means that certain sectors will be favored at the expense of others. In Jamaica, the manufacturing sector has been relatively favored in terms of the tax and expenditure policies of both the PNP and the JLP (see Danielson 1989) but the forms this support has taken differ between the two governments: although the

PNP intervened in the economy balancing high levels of taxes with high levels of subsidies, the JLP cut taxes as well as subsidies. Thus, for instance, although almost 35 percent of all tax revenue emanated from the manufacturing sector during the 1970s, only some 28 percent came from that source during the first four years of the JLP government (Danielson, 1993, 79).

Why is the manufacturing sector favored? The major explanation is that many influential interest groups are associated with that sector. Both the trade unions (from which the PNP receives large amounts of campaign money) and the producer interest groups (which are often eager supporters of the JLP) are firmly based in the manufacturing sector. Furthermore, for several reasons, it may be easier to organize interest groups and to influence policy formation in the manufacturing sector than in, say, the agricultural sector: production units in the former sector are fewer, larger and less geographically dispersed; the labor force is articulate and relatively skilled. In short, the costs of forming interest groups as identified by Olson (1965) are relevant here.[13]

The methods used to secure additional political support seem to have differed between the JLP and the PNP regimes. Although both have made extensive use of patronage, particularly when in power, the JLP of the 1980s has consistently argued for less public intervention in the economy and has consequently been less prone to manipulate the distribution of income through subsidies, tax concessions and price controls. The PNP strategy, on the other hand, was to collect large sums of tax revenue and to support certain groups both by direct spending (e.g., subsidies to the poor) and by expansion of public sector employment (Danielson, 1993, Chapter 6). Whereas the JLP relied on support from groups that would benefit from less government intervention, the PNP counted on increasing support from groups that would gain from redistribution either directly (low-income earners, import competing industrialists) or indirectly (actual or prospective government employees).

As has been noted, there was a certain consensus regarding trade policies during the 1960s. Although the JLP regime paid lip service to free trade, it also appreciated the political advantages of rapid industrialization and consequently attempted to build a domestic manufacturing sector behind tariff walls. Since the PNP as well advocated import substitution during the 1960s, trade policies were not debated much during that decade. However, after the PNP victory in 1972 things changed. Edward Seaga replaced Hugh Shearer as JLP leader in October 1974 and a harsh critique of the PNPs trade policies began almost immediately.[14]

Is it possible to discern any change in trade policies that may be due to the escalating critique and that consequently can be taken as an attempt of increasing the level of obfuscation? First, the prime objective of tariffs in Jamaica has always been to protect domestic industries. This, in a vote-maximizing framework, means that the target for favorization is not those that might benefit from extra tariff revenue, but those associated with import-competing industries. Also, the role that tariffs actually have as a source of revenue was significantly reduced in the second half of the 1970s (Ayub 1981, Chapter 3). Furthermore, the PNP government did not only lower tariff levels, it also increased the level of obfuscation in the sense of Magee, Brock and Young (1989) in that it resorted to other means of protection—notably quantitative restrictions. The number of goods under quantitative restrictions increased from 201 in 1973 to 334 in 1979; of the goods added to the restrictions list, the overwhelming majority were consumer goods (Ayub 1981, 33). As has been argued by Danielson and Lundahl (1992), a change in the public opinion regarding the social costs of a certain policy (possibly as a result of information from other parties) decreases the policy level—in this case, the average tariff rate. At the same time, however, the PNP government obviously resorted to obfuscation in that it substituted quantitative import restrictions for tariffs.

How can this be explained? One result in Danielson and Lundahl's (1992) model of policy formation in a democratic economy is that a change in the public opinion does not affect the level of obfuscation. However, after the forming of the PSoJ in 1976, PNP party officials (including Prime Minister Manley) were in close contact with representatives for the private sector businesses. At its initiation, the PSoJ elected Carlton Alexander—a firm supporter of the PNP and according to the ranking made by Stephens and Stephens (1986, Appendix 2) one of the most influential individuals in the private sector during the 1970s—as its president. Furthermore, the government formed a National Planning Committee with representatives from trade unions, private sector interest groups and the government (Stephens & Stephens 1986, 211). It is likely that Jamaican trade policies were on the agenda at some of the numerous meetings. Consequently, the increase in obfuscation with regard to trade policies may possibly be explained by increased lobby information; increased information to the lobby regarding the benefits of a more indirect policy leads to a higher level of optimal obfuscation in the Danielson and Lundahl model. The suggestion that the increase in obfuscation was intended to favor import competing industries is further substantiated by the fact that over 80 percent of the goods added to the restrictions list were consumer goods, and most of Jamaica's import competing and manufacturing industry produces such goods.

One of the basic problems for the PNP during the late 1970s and the entire 1980s was the insufficient party funds. As the party's commitment to democratic socialism increased toward the end of the 1970s, as the accusations from the opposition and the media for economic mismanagement increased, as political as well as non-political violence escalated—the number of murders increased from 152 in 1970 to 889 in 1980—and as economic conditions deteriorated at an accelerating pace, the private sector producers gradually turned away from the PNP and instead supported the JLP. The remaining supporters—mainly blue-collar labor, urban poor and part of the educated middle class—were not willing or able to support a costly administrative party apparatus, particularly not as elections drew closer.[15] Consequently, the PNP could no longer use the traditional means of patronage to reward loyal party workers. It became necessary to find other means. Since the party was in power, it had access to government revenue; this was used as a substitute for the lack of pecuniary contributions from supporting interest groups.

The strategy for rewarding loyal party workers was through employment. Such a policy could even be publicly justified with reference to the high rates of unemployment. The method was to allocate funds to public organizations and institutions in return for increased employment. Between 1976 and 1977 total government subsidies (measured in 1980 prices) more than tripled; during the entire period of PNP rule, the volume of government subsidies doubled each year—from J$53 million in 1972 to J$652.9 million in 1981 (Danielson 1993, 171). Some of these funds were directed to the public sector: public sector employment almost doubled between 1974 and 1977. A majority of those newly employed in the public sector seem to have been PNP supporters or PNP members (see Stephens & Stephens 1986, Chs. 5-6). Alternative methods included measures to reward loyal members, in particular the youth, in the rural areas. Thus for instance, the Project Food Farms were intended to train budding farmers on state farms in farming techniques; the best students were to be selected and permanently settled on the land. The farms were supposed to be self-financed through the sale of crops; however, even the first years saw tremendous losses. The major reason for the eventual failure of this program was patronage on the part of local PNP officials (Stephens and Stephens, 1986, 278): "Local MP's put pressure on the farm managers to admit their supporters to the program, even if these had no interest in farming whatsoever and even if the farms had sufficient personnel already. As a result the farms became a source of relief employment rather than centers for training and efficient production."

Similar problems can be traced in the failed Program Land Lease. Here, as well, patronage—or, as it is called in Jamaica, victimization—serves as a method of rewarding the loyal cadre and thus of increasing the probability of being reelected.

Although the PNP tried to channel public revenues to party members in an attempt to substitute for lacking financial support from the business sector, the JLP sometimes used more flagrant means for securing victory in the elections.[16] Mention has already been made of the Tivoli Gardens project; later, in 1983, the JLP government in a most strategic move ensured at least five more years in government by the use of what might be classified as fraud.

This event, usually known as the bogus election of 1983 was as follows. After the successful election of 1980, the JLP faced serious problems in the form of a faltering support from what used to be its strongest foothold: the private sector capitalists. In the 1980 campaign, the party promised immediate economic recovery, "deliverance" from economic mismanagement and "jingling" in people's pockets (Stephens and Stephens, 1986, 263). The major JLP slogan in the campaign was "the poor can't take no more." Up to late 1982, Carl Stone's regular polls showed that people believed that the JLP could manage the economy better than could the PNP (Stephens and Stephens 1986, Table A15; Stone 1982). However, as the economic situation in Jamaica worsened in late 1982, support for the JLP diminished markedly. In early 1983, polls showed for the first time in several years that people believed that things were better under the PNP than under the JLP.

The participation of the JLP government in the Grenada invasion in October 1983 diminished political support for the JLP even further and it seemed inevitable that the party should lose a forthcoming election. To make things worse, negotiations with the IMF indicated that Jamaica had failed the performance test and that a large devaluation would be necessary. The strategy of the JLP was to move fast. On 23 November, Prime Minister Edward Seaga announced that the government had agreed to a 77 percent devaluation due to failure of passing the performance test. The PNP condemned the devaluation and demanded the resignation of the Minister of Finance (also Seaga). The JLP used this demand as an excuse for calling snap elections on 25 November. Nomination Day was set to 29 November and the election to 15 December. The PNP boycotted the elections because the election list had not been updated since 1980, so the elections would disenfranchise everybody who came to voting age after the last election (and support for the PNPs was strongest among the young). The JLP won the elections before any votes were cast and was consequently given some respite before the next election (scheduled for 1988).

In this case, the JLP did not succeed in "buying votes" along the lines previously sketched. The primary reason, of course, is that the government was dependent on foreign loans to run its current affairs and the major source of these loans was the IMF which demanded that certain conditions should be met. The possibilities for the government to react to interest group pressure were consequently severely restricted; its only possibility was to extend the time to the next election.

By way of summary, politics in Jamaica is a rather inventive business. Several different methods are employed in the pursuit for votes, including fraud, patronage and gang violence. The country's political history (at least since 1962) abounds with examples of misuse of public funds, corruption, different forms of patronage and systematic favorization of certain (possibly party-loyal) groups. The problem is to find the facts: when it comes to obfuscation, the facts are—almost by definition—difficult to identify and interpret. However, the examples provided here should make it quite clear that Jamaican political parties are at least partly willing to act according to the wishes of influential interest groups and are not completely foreign to the idea of trying to hide the true social costs of these actions to the voters. This means that the Mamalakis story of sectoral clashes, staged by the government, may be an adequate representation of the situation in Jamaica.

SURPLUS DISTRIBUTION AND SECTORAL CLASHES

The theory of sectoral clashes and coalitions[17] is erected around the simple idea that the classical conflict in the economy—that between labor and capital—is not the only one of significance for the determination of growth and stagnation. Specifically, two additional sources of conflict are identified. First, it is possible that all income recipients in any given sector may find it potentially beneficial to coalesce to improve their situation. Thus, for instance, it may be rational for workers and capitalists in the manufacturing sector to work for protection of the manufacturing sector. If total income in the sector increases, the labor-capital conflict in that sector may be over-shadowed by the prospect of increasing the manufacturing sector's slice of the total income pie. Similarly, if the total income in a sector decreases, labor and capital may be united in their struggle to restore the sector's income share. This does not only imply that the classical conflict from time to time may be resting, but also— and this is perhaps more important—that a conflict may develop between sectors: if manufacturing income recipients are fighting for protection of the manufacturing industry, their struggle may be opposed by income recipients in the sectors that use manufactured goods as inputs in their production, and thus are interested in low prices of manufactured goods.

Second, which is partly a corollary to the conflict source previously mentioned, since the state is seldom a neutral agent in sectoral struggles, another potential source of conflict is that between the state and specific sectors. A state that has been pursuing, say, an import substituting policy and wishes to switch to a policy promoting, for example, agricultural exports is likely to run into conflict with the income recipients of the manufacturing sector. The way in which the conflict is fought—and, of course, the likely outcome—is to a large extent dependent on the relative economic and political strength of the combatants.

It is quite clear that a government that extracts taxes has an opportunity to favor one sector at the expense of others. Neo-classical theory theaches that the optimal way in which a certain amount of tax revenue is extracted is by equating the marginal social cost of taxation with the marginal social benefit (including any benefits from additional government expenditures following the increment in tax revenues) for all tax-payers. For this conclusion to have predictive value it is necessary that the government (i.e., the tax collector) is a neutral instrument whose exclusive interest is to improve "social welfare." Not many governments in the Third World are likely to fulfill this criterion.

One of Mamalakis' prime hypotheses is that the government is likely to support the manufacturing sector at the expense of agriculture and "foreign sectors"—typically extractive industries. This hypothesis conforms to the pattern well known from Africa and Latin America: import substitution, aimed to stimulation of domestic manufacturing production and discouragement of imports of manufactured goods. Some of the effects are equally well known: discrimination of agriculture in favor of manufacturing and labor in favor of capital, and the problem of bottlenecks, in particular concerning capital goods, raw materials and spare parts. What is less well known is why Third World governments continue to follow a policy that has been condemned by economists for at least two decades.

The persistence of governments to stay faithful to import substitution is often explained in terms of "non-economic" factors. Mamalakis (1969, 12-13) writes that

> Conviction of governments that industry is the *deus ex machina* in achieving growth . . . lead to the clash. . . . Development of sectors other than industry is either neglected or, in extreme cases, suppressed as having detrimental repercussions on industrial growth. Alba's statement that 'In Latin America a ready-made cure is always available. Today it is industrialization,' is less than an axiom but widely held not only in Latin America but also in other continents. . . . Revival of the industrialization doctrines that swept the European continent at the turn of the century and a depression theory of economic growth . . . started the trend. . . . In this context theories of balanced multi-sectoral growth were at best ignored, at worst systematically assailed; and the importance of foreign trade faded away. Industry became a symbol of development, achievement, prestige.[18]

It will be argued that import substitution (or, more precisely, favorization of the manufacturing sector) is an attractive policy not because—as is often argued—the existence and expansion of such a sector lends prestige to the government or because it would let the country escape the grips of neo-colonialism and imperialism. The manufacturing sector is favored simply because it is cheaper to tax that sector than it is to tax other sectors; and the government strives to maximize its tax revenues.

Why should the government attempt to maximize its revenues? The answer to that question is as simple: because if the government wishes to reallocate resources it is easier to do so by first collecting revenues and then spend them than it would be to use "incentives" and market forces for the reallocation process. If the government wishes to stimulate the production of, say, mangoes it is easier (although not necessarily less expensive) to do so by collecting taxes and providing subsidies to potential mango farmers, than it is to manipulate the relative price of mango (which might have a number of possibly undesirable secondary effects). But to collect the funds necessary, the government must, in the first phase, stimulate output and employment in sectors that are characterized by low costs of taxation. In the second phase, these funds can be used to stimulate whatever the government wishes to stimulate.

In the case of Jamaica, two relevant facts emerge. First, Jamaica has stimulated the expansion of the manufacturing sector since the mid 1950s. Two important incentive laws were passed in 1956—the Industrial Incentive Law and the Export Industry (Encouragement) Law. Both were designed to attract investment to the manufacturing sector. During the early years of the 1960s output in the manufacturing sector grew faster than overall output. Mahmood Ali Ayub (1981, 32) notes that the "performance of the manufacturing sector [between 1962 and 1967] was largely the result of a process of import substitution fostered initially by the industrial incentives." Similarly, Owen Jefferson (1971, 139) finds that about 57 percent of the expansion of the manufacturing sector between 1956 and 1966 can be attributed to the incentive legislation. After 1966, when the potential for "easy" or "primary" import substitution became less abundant, the rate of growth of the manufacturing sector slowed down, although quantitative restrictions became a supplement to tariffs as a means to control imports (Ayub, 1981, 32). Between 1966 and 1984 the amount of manufacturing goods available to Jamaicans declined by some 30 percent.[19] This suggests that although the protective part of the import substitution policy has worked as expected, the incentive part has failed: domestic production of manufactured goods has not increased as much as manufacturing imports have declined.

Second, tax revenues after 1974 have been dominated by incomes from the bauxite levy. From a value of some J$304 million in 1973 (17.5 percent of GDP), total tax revenues increased to J$597 million (22.8 percent of GDP) two years later; in 1974—the first year of the levy—revenues from the bauxite levy exceeded the revenues from income taxes by some J$4 million (NIP 1981, 10-11). Between 1973 and 1974, tax revenues from the mining sector increased sevenfold.[20] Although the main objective of the levy was to raise revenue, other factors cannot be ignored. Thus, for instance, taxation of a largely foreign-owned sector could be politically desirable for the relatively fresh and socialist-oriented Manley government. According to Mamalakis (1969, 24): "If a domestic and foreign-owned sector clash, overt discrimination of the foreign one can be a political asset and thus preferred." Whatever the real reasons were, the fact is that the Manley government was in desperate need of funds to be able to afford to expand social services.

During the PNP era (1972-80), government expenditures and involvement increased rapidly. State and co-operative ownership in the economy increased from 2 to over 20 percent (Stephens & Stephens 1986, 282), and between 1970 and 1977 government consumption increased from 12 to 22 percent of GDP

(Stone 1986, Table 2). After Manley's fall in 1980, government expenditures continued to be relatively high with a public consumption averaging some 20 percent of GDP.[21] Expenditures have continued to be financed out of tax revenues; in fact, since the Seaga government obviously seems to have been prepared to go very far to balance the budget, rates of taxation were increased. State involvement in the economy does not appear to have diminished after 1980. Carl Stone (1986, 117) notes that "by the early 1980s massive employment of temporary and special project staff who remained after projects completely swelled the size of ministries such as the Agricultural Ministry to a staff size of an estimated 10,000."

Together, the presented evidence appears to support the suggestion presented earlier: that apparent favorization of certain sectors (such as manufacturing industry) does not imply that the objective is to support these sectors per se, but rather to increase the extractable surplus. Mamalakis' theory thus seems to support one dimension of what really has occurred; but it ignores the real point, namely that the real objective is to increase tax revenues.

Given the rather plausible assumption that the structure of direct taxes does not differ between sectors, the government has at its disposition a number of means for discriminating between different sectors. These include, inter alia, indirect taxes, subsidies, and exchange rate and other relative price manipulations. In Jamaica it is clear that the manufacturing sector has been the subject of favorable treatment for a number of years. Apart from the evidence concerning import substitution that has been presented here, the exchange rate has been over-valued, implying that imports have been artificially cheap, which has promoted profitability in mining as well as in manufacturing (i.e., in the sectors using imported inputs); the Industrial Development Corporation has facilitated the development of new industries; part of the revenues from the bauxite levy has been used to set up a Capital Development Fund, aimed at promoting cheap credit for new manufacturing industries;[22] and so on.

These facts clearly point to the conclusion that the manufacturing sector has been favored by Jamaican governments. However, the material presented in Table 7.4 provides reason for some hesitation. The manufacturing sector is—apart from Mining—the sector in which the largest share of the surplus is appropriated by the government. Table 7.7 presents additional material that supports the previously derived conclusion.

It is clear from the table that Manufacturing generates a larger surplus per worker than the average sector in the economy. But although indirect taxes in the economy as a whole constitutes some 10 percent of total surplus, the corresponding value in the manufacturing sector is about 32 percent.

From the material in Tables 7.4 and 7.5 it is possible to make the following observations relevant for the hypothesis forwarded. (1) The share of profits in total surplus is lowest in the quasi-capital goods sectors. (2) The share of labor income in total surplus is lowest in consumption goods sectors. (3) The share of

Table 7.7
Distribution of Surplus Per Worker.
Manufacturing and Economy-Wide Average.
J$, 1975 Prices. Annual Averages.

	"Excess" Wages	Profits	Net Taxes	Total Surplus
1970-74				
Manufacturing	3,580.7	2,633.9	2,428.8	8,643.4
Total	3,247.6	2,454.6	654.5	6,365.7
1975-79				
Manufacturing	4,932.7	1,952.9	3,785.4	10,671.0
Total	3,247.7	2,324.7	614.6	6,187.0
1980-84				
Manufacturing	3,677.8	2,248.2	2,943.1	8,869.1
Total	2,995.5	2,259.3	658.6	5,913.4

Sources: Labor data: AAS (1971, Table 17); RLF (1980, 3-4); RLF (1984, 2-4). National accounts data: NIP (1981, Table 6); NIP (1984, Table 7).

taxes in total surplus increases during the first sub-period most rapidly in the quasi-capital goods sectors. This is almost entirely due to the implementation of the bauxite levy. Since the negative output effects of the levy became increasingly visible during the latter part of the 1970s and the early 1980s, revenues from this sector decline somewhat between the two latter subperiods. (4) During the entire period, taxation as a share of total surplus in the consumption goods sectors increases. Although less than one-fifth of the surplus in these sectors was extracted as net indirect taxes in 1970-74, only some three-quarters remained in the hands of firms and workers a decade later. Since virtually the entire surplus in the agricultural sector remains in private hands, it is—as is also demonstrated in Table 7.7—the manufacturing sector that carries the burden of increased taxation.

The material presented in this chapter thus paints a picture consisting of three stages.

Stage I: The government favors consumption goods sectors in general and manufacturing in particular. The means used are traditional import substitution tools: manipulation of the exchange rate, subsidies and the like. The funds to finance this favorization come from excessive taxation of exported goods—in particular bauxite and alumina.

Stage II: The government increases taxation of the consumption goods sectors. In terms of dollars per worker, it is most visible in the manufacturing sector, but the agricultural sector experiences a change in which a net subsidy per worker of some J$16 in 1970-74 is changed into a net tax of some J$16 in 1980-84 (NIP 1981, 52-53; NIP 1984, 36-37). During the latter half of the period, the burden of taxation shifts from capital goods sectors to consumption goods sectors. One plausible reason for this change in the pattern of taxation is that the possibilities of taxing quasi-capital goods sectors have been more or less exhausted, due to a contraction of output. Furthermore, it is likely that the initial stimulation of the consumption goods sectors was guided by considerations concerning the costs of surplus extraction.[23]

Stage III: The additional tax revenue collected from the consumption goods sectors is used to finance an expansion of the service sectors and, in particular, the government sector. Space limits prevent discussing the reasons for this expansion here.[24] Since it is the government sector that accounts for the bulk of the service sector's expansion, it might be suggested, however, that one important reason probably is lack of confidence in "the market mechanism" and trust in the government's talents for efficient resource reallocation.

CONCLUDING REMARKS

It has been suggested in this chapter that changes in the sectoral and functional distribution of the surplus to some extent reflect the wishes of the government. In particular, it has been asserted that the apparently irrational loyalty toward import substitution policies has a logical explanation if it is assumed (1) that the government has little confidence in the market mechanism, (2) that the government has a high regard concerning its own abilities to reallocate resources efficiently and (3) that the costs of surplus extraction are relatively low in the manufacturing sector.

Official statement is one thing; realpolitik another. Although it should be no surprise that the Manley government attempted to attain a higher degree of state involvement in the economy, and to expand state enterprises, it might be unexpected to find the "conservative" Seaga government continuing the protective, high-tax policy of the 1970s. The expressed objectives of the Seaga government included, inter alia, increased reliance on the market mechanism and although "state intervention in the economy would not actually be reduced back to the pre-1972 level, ... there was an explicit commitment ... to investigate divestment of all state enterprises other than utilities" (Stephens & Stephens 1986, 252). The material presented in this chapter does not suggest that state involvement in the Jamaican economy has been curtailed after 1980.

NOTES

1. This statement requires an explanation. The problem of surplus method consists mainly of a reasonable definition of "subsistence." As seen in Chapter 3, most authors follow Baran (1957) in using the concept "essential consumption," which does not lend itself to a straightforward interpretation. The issue, then, boils down to the question of

whether part of wages is surplus or not. The observation made in the text is simply based on the data in Table 5.2: if market wages are defined as essential consumption (so labor does not receive any surplus), the sum of profit and taxes would constitute the surplus. With this very generous definition of subsistence, surplus would still constitute approximately 50 percent of net domestic production.

2. The "new institutional economics" and the "new political economy" emanate from important research on transaction costs and institutions in the 1960s on the one hand and "public choice" on the other. Important contributions, drawing heavily on Anne O. Krueger's (1974) seminal work include Nabli and Nugent (1989), North (1990), Findlay (1991), Meier (1991) and the collection by Colander (1984). A well-balanced survey of the study of institutions is Eggertsson (1990) and Magee et al. (1989) survey the economic approach to the study of political processes and the state. Rowley et al. (1988) is a fine collection of articles on rent-seeking.

3. Mainstream macroeconomic theory is just beginning to appreciate the importance of credibility. See Persson and Tabellini (1990) for a survey.

4. The particular forms favorization take depends, of course, on what groups or sectors the government chooses to support.

5. Mamalakis (1971).

6. See JBI (1984) for a full analysis of the construction and consequences of this tax.

7. See, for instance, NIP (1984, 36-37) where it is shown that the subsidies to the distribution sector in current prices vary between J$139 million (1978) and J$1.5 million (1983).

8. NIP (1984, 37).

9. Ayub (1981, Ch. 2) provides a critical account of the incentives legislation.

10. These have been calculated as the arithmetic average, using the sectors' share of GDP as weights, that is, if a and m stand for, respectively, output in fixed prices in the agricultural and manufacturing sector, and if PS_a and PS_m denote the shares of the sectoral surpluses accruing to private actors in these sectors, the private share of the surplus in the consumption goods sector equals

(n7.1)
$$\frac{a}{a+m} \times PS_a + \frac{m}{a+m} \times PS_m.$$

11. See Stone (1981, 207-210) for a classification of voters into safe and marginal. In the elections between 1959 and 1976, eight parishes are classified as stable (six for the PNP and two for the JLP) and six are classified as unstable (Stone 1981, Table 1).

12. In one of the polling stations in Tivoli Gardens, 83 persons voted for Seaga although only there were only 82 electors on the voters' list (of course, nobody voted for Dudley Thompson, Seaga's opponent). In an adjoining polling station, Seaga got 75 votes from 74 electors. In the campaign before the election, Seaga gave support to youth gangs and is alleged to have introduced guns into the Jamaican political debate. This, along with his other merits earned him the title of "Minister of Devilment and Warfare" (Stephens and Stephens 1986, 46; Lacey 1977, 49).

13. See also Magee (1990) for some empirical estimates of lobbying and rent-seeking.

14. See Miller (1981) for a comparative analysis of the major issues in the 1967 and the 1976 elections and Stephens and Stephens (1986, Chapters 3-4) for a detailed account of the reactions of the opposition.

15. See Stephens and Stephens (1986, 265-267, 304-305) for a detailed account of the deteriorating financial situation of the PNP.

16. See Stephens and Stephens (1986, Chapters 2-3) and Kaufman (1985, Chapters 1-4) or Stone (1988, 43-64) for a discussion of the JLP strategy in the 1960s.

17. Developed in Mamalakis (1969) and completely revised in Mamalakis (1971). See also the appended comments in *Latin American Research Review*, 1971, Vol. 6.

18. The reference to Alba is Alba (1961, 45).

19. Calculated from Gafar and Napier (1978, 98) and NIP (1984, 16). All values have been deflated to 1975 prices using the implicit GDP deflator in IMF (1986, 416-417).

20. Kaufman (1985, 83) and Stephens and Stephens (1986, 79).

21. Comparing 1976-79 with 1980-83. Data from NIP (1984, 4-5; 10-11).

22. Details are provided by Hughes (1984).

23. Danielson (1993, Ch. 2) contains a simple model of the sectoral pattern of taxation in the presence of collection costs.

24. Mamalakis (1971), however, suggests that the increasing demands for services from the growing middle class may stimulate increased service production. See also Danielson and Lundahl (1992) and Danielson (1993) in which the main thesis is that the government attempts to increase the probability of remaining in power by expanding public sector employment.

IV

Concluding Observations

8

Is Surplus Obsolete?

Although surplus constituted a core concept in economic theory from the Physiocrats until the height of Classical Political Economy, it went into obscurity with the rise to dominance of neoclassical theory. Despite the facty that some signs of revival for surplus became visible after the Second World War, it would probably not be unfair to paraphrase Keynes in saying that the concept of surplus has only lived on, furtively, below the surface, in the underworlds of Piero Sraffa or Paul Baran.

Although recent surplus approaches have most often been associated with dissatisfaction with contemporary mainstream theory, this is, of course not a necessary condition for using the concept. As the present work has attempted to demonstrate, it is perfectly possible to construct a surplus concept that can be used in harmony with (in this case) development theory.

To claim that "surplus"—unless it is juxtaposed with Marshallian consumer or producer surplus—is simply a reflection of underlying market imperfections is to gravely misunderstand the concept—at least as it has been used in this study. As has been repeatedly stated, it is all a matter of definitions. Pick your choice of output—national income, gross national product, net domestic product. Take one part of that and call it "subsistence." Then the remainder is called "surplus." A basic problem in this approach is not to "prove" the existence of a surplus, but to choose "subsistence" in a manner compatible with economic theory. In this work, "subsistence" relies on the Lewis model of the dual economy; it thus seems as if it would be difficult to claim that the basis of this definition dwells in the underworlds of theory, far from accepted truth or established doctrines.

The significance of a concept derived from an identity depends of course on the object of study. Although "surplus" measures something that is not measured by "consumption" or "output," it is not necessarily superior to these. It depends on the questions asked. Surely, if total annual income in an economy is to be examined, GNP is more appropriate than GDP.[1] The relevance of any definition of surplus, therefore, is not determined by whether critics acknowledge its existence or not, but whether the issues that can be studied by aid of the concept are interesting. This is the crux of the matter.

The surplus concept as it has been outlined in this study reflects income differentials. To say that the surplus for any one year equalled 30,000 does not reveal much. On the other hand, to say that the surplus in fixed prices changed from 30,000 to 35,000 is to say either that the value of total output has increased or that the distribution of income has changed at the expense of agricultural labor, or both. Hence insofar as it is useful to link directly a concept of total output (such as, say, GDP) to the distribution of income with special attention paid to wage incomes in agriculture, the concept of surplus is indeed relevant.

The objective of this study as far as "surplus" as a theoretical construct is concerned has been twofold. First, it has attempted to develop a definition, free from some of the flaws found in other concepts and, second, to demonstrate how "surplus" can be used to illuminate redistributional processes in an underdeveloped economy. Admittedly, there is some skewness in the study concentrating, perhaps excessively, on state-governed redistribution. This bias is conscious and a result of Jamaica being the case study. Had a country with a less active government been analyzed, it is by no means certain that the lion's share of Part II would have been devoted to analysis of government actions. The sympathetic reader might perhaps interpret this in terms of flexibility of the surplus concept.

Three definitions of the surplus have been provided—four, if one counts the sectoral definition separately. The three that have been labeled S_I, S_{II} and S_{III} are logically connected. Although it is rather clear that S_{II} gives a more appropriate description of the distribution of the surplus than does S_I, it is equally clear that the latter is as close a representation as possible of the "original" distribution of the surplus—that is to say, it describes, with some important qualifications imposed by the data material, the distribution of the surplus prior to the government's redistributional policies. Hence, changes in the government's redistributional policies are necessarily reflected in the development of S_{II} relative to S_I.

The rationale for including S_{III} is quite different. A distinction that sank into the underworlds of theory with the rise of neoclassical theory is that between "productive" and "unproductive" activities. Here, S_{III} includes in the surplus subsistence payments to all publicly employed—including teachers, administrators and members of the secret police. As explained in Chapter 3, it may seem tempting to divide governmental activities into, as it were, "desirable" and "undesirable" activities (which, presumably, would leave the secret police in the latter category). Apart from the immense statistical difficulties inherent in this approach (for it is not at all certain that the researcher's demarcation between "desirable" and "undesirable" coincides with the categorization employed by the statistical authorities), the approach taken in this work is that normative analysis is better left to welfare economics. Surplus III measures what actually remains of output after depreciation allowances and subsistence payments to the productive labor force have been deducted.[2] There is no judgment whether the activities pursued by the government are "desirable" or not: S_{III} is simply an attempt to measure what in some sense might be interpreted as the "investable surplus."

Although at first glance it may appear as a weakness of "surplus" that not a single definition has been used through out the work, it is not. Again, it is important to choose the tools with respect to the problem under scrutiny; and it would certainly be foolish to stubbornly stick to a single definition when it is obvious that different definitions throw light on different issues. Furthermore, when it is realized that the definitions are closely interrelated (and, in a sense, are "derived" from the definition of S_I) the objection that more than one definition is used loses much, if not all, of its force.

Although the empirical part of this study is limited to studying a single economy during a relatively long period of time it would, of course, also be possible to analyze the relations between surplus and other macroeonomic magnitudes in a cross-sectional framework. Since the received view seems to be that, in a growing economy, the share of the labor force in agriculture declines faster than agriculture's share of output, agricultural labor productivity (and presumably agricultural wages) increases during secular, economy-wide growth.[3] How does the share of the surplus in GDP in rich countries compare to the share of the surplus in poor ones? Are there any significant differences in the distribution and disposal of the surplus among countries of different levels of income or, more importantly, is it possible to relate specific patterns of distribution and disposal of the surplus to certain levels of income? These important issues can be analyzed in a cross-sectional, surplus framework. Furthermore, the very construction of the concept ensures that data is relatively abundant.[4]

The bulk of this study has, however, been concerned with the development of the surplus in a single economy over the course of 22 years. Although data were available prior to 1962, it seemed natural to start the investigation at independence. As was noted, there has been—perhaps unduly—a bias toward the examination of the government's methods of surplus extraction. Two major points have been made.

First, the methods of surplus extraction available to the government can be classified as direct and indirect. The line of demarcation is drawn with respect to whether the method directly increases the government's share of the surplus or not.

Second, it is possible that the government combines these methods of extraction to increase its own share of the surplus. The number of possible combinations of direct and indirect methods is quite large. There are, however, some that seem to explain apparently irrational features in the economy. Thus, for instance, the combination of quantitative restrictions on manufacturing imports (which is an indirect method, since it transfers surplus to the manufacturing sector) with relatively high indirect taxes on domestic manufacturing production transfers—as has been demonstrated—surplus from other sectors to the manufacturing sector and from the manufacturing sector to the government. Hence, the existence of differentiated costs of surplus extraction may explain why import substitution continues to be an attractive policy for many governments, despite its well-known discouraging effects on other sectors.

Chapters 5 to 7 have been concerned with different aspects of surplus in Jamaica. To be specific, Chapter 5 dealt with the economy-wide surplus and its relation to savings and investment, Chapter 6 analyzed the macroeconomic consequences of surplus redistribution, whereas Chapter 7 used the framework of "sectoral clashes" to examine the sectoral distribution and redistribution of the surplus.

Surplus in Jamaica has increased throughout the period under study. This is true regardless of whether surplus is measured in volume terms, as share of GDP or per worker. Noteworthy is also that the pattern of change for, say, Surplus III per worker is rather different from Net Domestic Product (NDP) per worker. This fact should preclude any suspicions that "surplus" is simply a constant share of NDP, which does not reveal anything about economic realities that is not also reflected in NDP or GDP. On the contrary, Table 5.5 reveals that since surplus per worker fell at a slower rate than GDP per capita in the 1970s, a significant redistribution of income took place during the same period. Specifically, this means that subsistence payments increased during the period, which—in this particular case—should be interpreted as an increase in the average agricultural wage relative to GDP.

The distribution of the surplus has changed as well. Specifically, the following changes have been regarded as most important. First, labor's share of the economy-wide surplus has increased significantly, in particular with respect to the earnings of publicly employed labor. This means, essentially, that although the government has extracted increasing shares of the surplus, most of it has been used to expand the public labor force. In an economy-wide framework, this is reflected in an increase in labor's share of the surplus.

Second, the share of surplus accruing to labor has increased at the expense of profit; as demonstrated in Table 5.6, this decline is significant, amounting to some 25 percent between 1962-66 and 1982-84. This redistribution seems to be the major explanation for the rapid fall in private savings encountered during the 1970s. Resources were transferred to manufacturing from other sectors in the economy and further transferred (via increased indirect taxation) to the government. This affected incomes of firms and labor negatively. Since government expenditures to a large extent were used to finance expanding public employment, labor, as a functional income category, did not suffer. Incomes were thus transferred from firms to the government whose expenditures, however, grew at a rate far exceeding that of revenues. Since the propensity to save out of profit income exceeded that out of wage income, the result was that private savings declined and, of course, an increasing share of investments had to be financed out of "foreign savings."

Why, then, did the government's expenditure take on an increasing rate of growth in the early 1970s? These wider issues have not been given any detailed treatment in the text, but is seems likely that the answer may be found in the stated objectives of the new government entering power in 1972. The PNP was during the 1970s "democratic socialist," which means essentially four things.[5] First, the market economy was seen as unstable if left to itself, so more intervention than what would be suggested by simple efficiency considerations was considered desirable. In terms of expenditures, this implied, first, that funds were transferred from the government to firms or sectors for which stimulation was thought appropriate and, second, that utilities were priced below cost in order to increase the availability of these. Second, the democratic socialist party gave high priority to "social goods" such as education, health care and housing. This also explains why the public labor force expanded as rapidly as it did.

Third, the manufacturing sector was favored both with respect to other domestic sectors and with respect to imports. Although tariffs has never been a major means of raising revenue in Jamaica, quantitative restrictions are frequently used to control imports (Ayub 1981). With respect to the domestic intersectoral distribution of the surplus, the manufacturing sector was favored by the use of subsidies and biased domestic price relations—which is a consequence of the import substitution policy.

Fourth and finally, it is interesting and somewhat surprising to note the size of the surplus—in particular in relation to the volume of domestically generated savings. Chapter 5 showed that the size of the surplus amounts to some 80per cent of GDP and surplus per worker, in 1975 prices, did not for a single year fall below J$2,400 annually. In other words, provided that all members of the employed labor force were granted a wage equal to the average annual wage and that deductions for capital used up in the production process were properly made, there would still remain resources, amounting to approximately four-fifths of GDP that could be used for either consumption or saving. It goes without saying that the disposal of that surplus is of immense importance for the economy. The sad fact, however, seems to be that the major part of the surplus was not used to expand productive capacity. Nor does it appear from the analysis that substantial amounts of resources have been used, through the government's care, to improve the living conditions, directly or indirectly, of the not so well off. As the following example indicates, most of the surplus resources have gone to consumption—and, in particular, consumption of imported goods.

Making the quite bold assumption that private domestic savings are made entirely by firms, the figures presented in Chapter 5 reveal that on the average, less than 25 percent of profits, net of depreciation allowances, are saved and the trend is declining: from a little over 40 percent in the early 1960 to some 12 percent in the late 1970s.[6]

Recall from Chapter 2, however, that the classical theory was founded on the dual hypothesis that economic growth is determined by the size *and* the disposal of the economic surplus. In the light of the analysis of Chapter 5 this is more interesting. Combining the declining private propensity to save with the redistributional results reported earlier, one arrives at a conclusion that suggests that surplus was redistributed in favor of groups having higher than average marginal propensities to consume import goods and lower than average propensities to save. As seen, the principal beneficiaries of the government's redistributional policies were labor employed in the public sector. Furthermore, the data reported by Danielson (1990, Table 1) suggest that the wage rate in the public sector, throughout the period, was higher than wages in most other sectors of the economy. Hence, the beneficiaries of the policies were the middle income recipients, or—using income as a crude measure of class—the "middle class."

In sum, then, is it possible to state that the surplus analysis is relevant with respect to Jamaica's experience during the period 1962-84? Although an unqualified yes would be somewhat misleading, it is also not possible to reject the approach completely. This study has emphasized a number of features not generally analyzed in studies of Jamaica. These include government's methods of resource transfer and the intermediary role of sectors characterized by low transaction costs in the redistributive process. The analysis of these features does not, of course, require a surplus concept. However, there is a logic in combining "surplus" as the principal analytical concept with analysis of extraction and redistribution. Since the pattern of extraction to some extent is determined by the sectoral difference in transaction costs, low-cost sectors will be favored at the expense of high-cost sectors. Since agriculture is frequently characterized by relatively high costs of surplus extraction, it is not infrequently disfavored relative to other sectors, such as manufacturing. The particular definition of surplus employed in this study relates the sectoral distribution of income (and hence, in a sense, the relative "standard of living" in the agricultural sector) to total incomes. As far as the government favors sectors characterized by low costs of surplus extraction, therefore, it seems that "surplus" is a potentially useful concept in development studies.

NOTES

1. However, both these concepts—and indeed surplus as well—suffer from the familiar deficiencies associated with economic statistics in general and statistics in underdeveloped countries in particular. See, for instance Seers (1976, 135; 1983).

2. "Productive" as explained in Chapter 3, means "privately employed".

3. See, for instance, Yotopoulos and Nugent (1976, Ch. 16).

4. A preliminary survey reveals that the size, distribution and disposal of S_{III} could be calculated for 25 countries during the entire time period 1977-84 using the data in the UN's *Yearbook of National Account Statistics* and the ILO's *Yearbook of Labour Statistics* only.

5. Excellent accounts of the Manley period, both in terms of actual experience and in terms of ideology, are provided by Kaufman (1985) and Stephens and Stephens (1986).

6. Data comes from AAS (1963, 42), NIP (1981, 18), NIP (1984, 23) and IMF (1986, 416-417).

References

AAS (1963). *Annual Abstract of Statistics, 1963*. Kingston: Department of Statistics.

AAS (1968). *Annual Abstract of Statistics, 1968*. Kingston: Department of Statistics.

AAS (1969). *Annual Abstract of Statistics, 1969*. Kingston: Department of Statistics.

AAS (1971). *Annual Abstract of Statistics, 1971*. Kingston: Department of Statistics.

Alba, V. (1961). "The Latin American Style and the New Social Forces" in A. O. Hirschman (ed.): *Latin American Issues. Essays and Comments*, New York, NY: Twentieth Century Fund.

Allais, M. (1987). "The Equimarginal Principle: Meaning, Limits, and Generalization" *Rivista Internazionale di Scienze Economiche e Commerciali*, Vol. 34: 689-750.

Arrate, J. and L. Geller (1971). "Economic Surplus and the Budget" in K. Griffin (ed.): *Financing Development in Latin America*. London: Macmillan.

Ayub, M. A. (1981). *Made in Jamaica. The Development of the Manufacturing Sector*. Baltimore, MD: Johns Hopkins University Press.

Balassa, B. (1981). *The Newly Industrializing Countries in the World Economy*. New York, NY: Pergamon Press.

Baran, P. (1957). *The Political Economy of Growth*. New York, NY: Monthly Review.

Baran, P. (1970). "Economic Progress and Economic Surplus" in P. A. Baran (ed.): *The Longer View*. New York, NY: Monthly Review.

Baran, P. and P. Sweezy (1966). *Monopoly Capital*. New York, NY: Monthly Review.

Bardhan, P. (1993). "Economics of Development and the Development of Economics" *Journal of Economic Perspectives*, Vol. 7: 129-142.

Baumol, W. (1959). *Economic Dynamics*. London: Macmillan.

Bernal, R. M. Figueroa and M. Witter (1984). "Caribbean Economic Thought: The Critical Tradition" *Social and Economic Studies*, Vol. 33: 5-96.

Bien, Y. (1972). "The Contribution and Role of Taiwan's Agriculture in the Process of Economic Development" *Taiwan Bank Quarterly*, Vol. 23: 13-41.

Blaug, M. (1978). *Economic Theory in Retrospect*. Third edition. Cambridge: Cambridge University Press.

Bleaney, M. (1976). *Underconsumption Theories. A History and Critical Analysis.* London: Lawrence & Wishart.

Blomqvist, Å. (1986). "The Economics of Price Scissors: Comment" *American Economic Review*, Vol. 76: 1188-1191.

Boserup, E. (1965). *The Conditions of Agricultural Growth.* Chicago, IL: Aldine.

Boss, H. (1990). *Theories of Surplus and Transfer. Parasites and Producers in Economic Thought.* London: Unwin Hyman.

Boyd, D. A. C. (1985). "Jamaica: Pay As You Earn Taxation" *Caribbean Finance and Management*, Vol. 1: 5-16.

Boyd, D. A. C. (1988). *Economic Management, Income Distribution and Poverty in Jamaica.* Westport, CT: Praeger.

Broome, J. (1983). *The Microeconomics of Capitalism.* New York, NY: Academic Press.

Caravale, G. A. and D. A. Tosato (1980). *Ricardo and the Theory of Value, Distribution and Growth*, London: Routledge and Kegan Paul.

Carter, M. R. (1986). "The Economics of Price Scissors: Comment" *American Economic Review*, Vol. 76: 1192-1194.

Chenery, H. B. (1979). *Structural Change and Development Policy.* New York, NY: Oxford University Press.

Chevannes, B. (1981). "The Rastafari and the Urban Youth" in C. Stone and A. Brown (eds.): *Perspectives on Jamaica in the Seventies.* Kingston: Jamaica Publishing House.

Colander, D. C. (1984). *Neoclassical Political Economy.* Cambridge, MA: Ballinger.

Craven, J. (1979). *The Distribution of the Product.* London: George Allen & Unwin.

Danielson, A. (1986). *Aspects of Industrialization in Jamaica.* MFS-study #2. Lund: Department of Economics, University of Lund.

Danielson, A. (1989). "La Lucha Por El Excedente: Jamaica, 1970-84" in M. Lundahl and W. Pelupessy (eds.): *Crisis Economica en Centroamerica y el Caribe.* San José: Editorial DEI.

Danielson, A. (1990). "The Economic Surplus. Formation, Distribution and Role in Economic Growth" *Social and Economic Studies*, Vol. 39: 127-152.

Danielson, A. (1993). *The Political Economy of Development Finance. Public Sector Expansion and Economic Development in Jamaica.* Boulder, CO: Westview Press.

Danielson, A. and M. Lundahl (1992). *Endogenous Policy Formation and the Principle of Optimal Obfuscation. Theory and Some Evidence from Haiti and Jamaica.* Paper presented at the Eastern Economic Association meeting, New York, NY, March.

Dasgupta, A. K. (1985): *Epochs of Economic Theory*, Oxford: Basil Blackwell.

Davies, O. (1984). *An Analysis of Jamaica's Fiscal Budget (1974-83) With Special Reference to the Impact of the Bauxite Levy.* Department of Economics Occasional Paper Series, # 2. Kingston: ISER, University of the West Indies.

Davis, J. B. (1992). *The Economic Surplus in Advanced Economies.* London: Edward Elgar.

Dawson, M. and J. B. Foster (1992). "The Tendency of the Surplus to Rise, 1963-1988" in J. B. Davis (ed.): *The Economic Surplus in Advanced Economies*. London: Edward Elgar.

Deane, P. (1978): *The Evolution of Economic Ideas*, Cambridge: Cambridge University Press.

Dixit, A. K. (1969). "Marketable Surplus and Dual Development" *Journal of Economic Theory*, Vol. 1: 203-219.

Eggertsson, T. (1990). *Economic Behavior and Institutions*. Cambridge: Cambridge University Press.

Ekelund, R. B. and R. F. Hebert (1975). *A History of Economic Theory and Method*. New York: McGraw-Hill.

Eltis, W. (1975a). "François Quesnay: A Reinterpretation. 1. The *Tableau Économique*" *Oxford Economic Papers*, Vol 27: 167-200.

Eltis, W. (1975b). "François Quesnay: A Reinterpretation. 2. The Theory of Economic Growth" *Oxford Economic Papers*, Vol 27: 327-351.

Eltis, W. (1984). *The Classical Theory of Economic Growth*. London: Macmillan.

Erlich, A. (1950). "Preobrazhensky and the Economics of Soviet Industrialization" *Quarterly Journal of Economics*, Vol. 64: 57-88.

External Trade, Kingston: The Statistical Institute of Jamaica. Annual.

Fei, J. C. H. and G. Ranis (1964). *Development of the Labor Surplus Economy. Theory and Policy*. Homewood, IL: Irwin.

Findlay, R. (1973). *International Trade and Development Theory*. New York, NY: Columbia University Press.

Findlay, R. (1991). "The New Political Economy: Its Explanatory Power for LDCs" in G. M. Meier (ed.): *Politics and Policy Making in Developing Countries*. San Francisco, CA: International Center for Economic Growth.

Fishman, L. (1992). "Economic Surplus and the Market System" in J. B. Davis (ed.): *The Economic Surplus in Advanced Economies*. London: Edward Elgar.

Foley, V. (1973). "An Origin of the Tableau Economique" *History of Political Economy*, Vol. 5: 121-150.

Gafar, J. and W. J. Napier (1978). *Trends and Patterns of Commonwealth Caribbean Trade, 1954-1970*. Kingston: ISER, University of the West Indies.

Gayle, D. J. (1986). *The Small Developing State*. Aldershot: Gower.

Gersowitz, M. (1988). "Saving and Development" in H. B. Chenery and T. N. Srinivasan (eds.): *Handbook of Development Economics, Vol 1*. Amsterdam: North-Holland.

Girvan, N. (1970). *Foreign Capital and Economic Underdevelopment in Jamaica*. Kingston: ISER, University of the West Indies.

Girvan, N. R. Bernal and W. Hughes (1980). "The IMF and the Third World: The Case of Jamaica, 1974-1980" *Development Dialogue*, No. 2: 113-155.

Goodwin, R. (1970). *Elementary Economics From the Higher Standpoint*. Cambridge: Cambridge University Press.

Griffin, K. (1971). "Introduction" in K. Griffin (ed.): *Financing Development in Latin America*, London: Macmillan.

Harcourt, G. (1972). *Some Cambridge Controversies in the Theory of Capital*. Cambridge: Cambrige University Press.

Harris, J. R. and M. P. Todaro (1970). "Migration, Unemployment and Development: A Two-Sector Analysis" *American Economic Review*, Vol. 60: 126-142.

Hicks, J. R. (1965): *Capital and Growth*, Oxford: Clarendon Press.

Hicks, J. R. (1976) "'Revolutions' in Economics" in S. Latsis (ed.): *Method and Appraisal in Economics*. Cambridge: Cambridge University Press.

Hope, K. R. (1987). *Development Finance and the Development Process*. London: Greenwood Press.

Hornby, J. M. (1968). "Investment and Trade Policy in the Dual Economy" *Economic Journal*, Vol. 78: 96-107.

Hughes, W. (1984). "Mineral Taxation and Economic Development: The Use of Jamaica's Production Levy Earnings 1973-84" *The JBI Journal*, Vol. 3: 65-82.

IMF (1986). *International Financial Statistics, Yearbook, 1986*. Washington DC: The International Monetary Fund.

IMF (1988). *International Financial Statistics, Yearbook, 1988*. Washington DC: The International Monetary Fund.

Ishikawa, S. (1967). "Resource Flow Between Agriculture and Industry: The Chinese Experience" *The Developing Economies*, Vol. 5: 118-145.

IYTS (1965). *International Yearbook of Trade Statistics 1965*, Geneva: United Nations.

IYTS (1969). *International Yearbook of Trade Statistics 1969*, Geneva: United Nations.

IYTS (1975). *International Yearbook of Trade Statistics 1975*, Geneva: United Nations.

IYTS (1978). *International Yearbook of Trade Statistics 1978*, Geneva: United Nations.

JBI (1984). "Mineral Resource Taxation with Reflections on the Jamaican Bauxite Production Levy" *Jamaican Bauxite Institute's Journal*, Vol. 3. Special issue.

Jefferson, O. (1971). *The Post-War Economic Development of Jamaica*. Kingston: ISER: University of the West Indies.

Kaldor, N. (1960). "Alternative Theories of Distribution" in Kaldor, N: *Essays on Value and Distribution*. London: Duckworth.

Kaldor, N. (1964). "Economic Problems of Chile" in *Essays on Economic Policy, II*. London: Duckworth.

Kanth, R. (1987). "Against Surplus Theorising: A Comment" *Review of Radical Political Economics*, Vol. 19: 83-85.

Kaufman, M. (1985). *Jamaica under Manley. Dilemmas of Socialism and Democracy*. London: Zed Press.

Keynes, J. M. (1936). *The General Theory of Employment, Interest and Money*. London: Macmillan.

King, B. B. (1985). "What is a SAM?" in G. Pyatt and J. I. Round (eds.): *Social Accounting Matrices. A Basis for Planning*. Washington DC: The World Bank.

Kirkpatrick, C. H. and F. I. Nixon (1984). "Industrial Structure, International Trade and Development" in C. H. Kirkpatrick, N. Lee and F. I. Nixon (eds.): *Industrial*

Structure and Policy in Less Developed Countries. London: George Allen & Unwin.

Kregel, J. A. (1975). *The Reconstruction of Political Economy. An Introduction to Post-Keynesian Economics*. London: Macmillan.

Krueger, A. O. (1974). "The Political Economy of the Rent-Seeking Society" *American Economic Review*, Vol. 64: 291-303.

Kuznets, S. (1961). "Economic Growth and the Contribution of Agriculture: Notes on Measurement" *International Journal of Agrarian Affairs*, Vol. 3: 68-81.

Lacey, T. (1977). *Violence and Politics in Jamaica, 1960-70*. Manchester: Manchester University Press.

Levi, J. F. S. (1976/77). "Population Pressure and Agricultural Change in the Land-Intensive Economy" *Journal of Development Studies*, Vol. 13: 61-78.

Lewis, W. A. (1944). "An Economic Plan for Jamaica" *Agenda*, Vol. 3: 1-13.

Lewis, W. A. (1950a). "Industrial Development in Puerto Rico" *Caribbean Economic Review*, Vol. 2: 98-112.

Lewis, W. A. (1950b). "The Industrialisation of the British West Indies" *Caribbean Economic Review*, Vol. 2: 204-231.

Lewis, W. A. (1954). "Economic Development with Unlimited Supplies of Labour" *Manchester School of Social and Economic Studies*, Vol. 22: 139-191.

Lewis, W. A. (1972). "Reflections on Unlimited Labor" in L. E. diMarco (ed.): *International Economics and Development. Essays in Honor of Raúl Prebisch*. New York, NY: Academic Press.

Lewis, W. A. (1976). "Development and Distribution" in A. Cairncross and M. Puri (eds.): *Employment, Distribution and Development Strategy. Essays in Honour of H. W. Singer*. London: Macmillan.

Lewis, W. A. (1984). "Development Economics in the 1950s" in Meier G. M. and D. Seers (eds.): *Pioneers in Development*. Oxford: Oxford University Press.

Lewis, W. A. (1988). "The Roots of Development Theory" in H. Chenery and T. N. Srinivasan (eds.): *Handbook of Development Economics, Vol. 1*. Amsterdam: North-Holland.

Lichtenstein, P. (1983). *An Introduction to Post-Keynesian and Marxian Theories of Value and Price*. London: Macmillan.

Lippit, V. (1985). "The Concept of the Surplus in Economic Development" *Review of Radical Political Economics*, Vol. 17: 1-19.

Lippit, V. (1992). "Reevaluating the Concept of Surplus" in J. B. Davis (ed.): *The Economic Surplus in Advanced Economies*. London: Edward Elgar.

Lipton, M. (1977). *Why Poor People Stay Poor. Urban Bias in World Development*. London: Temple Smith.

Magee, S. P. (1990). "Cross National Estimates of Rent Seeking, Tariffs and Voter Rationality in Political-Economic General Equilibrium." University of Texas at Austin, mimeo.

Magee, S. P. W. A. Brock and L. Young (1989). *Black Hole Tariffs and Endogenous Policy Theory*, Cambridge: Cambridge University Press.

Mamalakis, M. (1969). "The Theory of Sectoral Clashes" *Latin American Research Review*, Vol. 4: 1-31.

Mamalakis, M. (1971). "The Theory of Sectoral Clashes and Coalitions Revisited" *Latin American Research Review*, Vol. 6: 103-141.

Mankiw, N. G. (1990). "A Quick Refresher Course in Macroeconomics" *Journal of Economic Literature*, Vol. 28: 1645-1660.

Manley, M. (1976). *The Search for Solutions*. Oshawa: Maple House.

Manley, M. (1982). *Jamaica: Struggle in the Periphery*. Oxford: Third World Media Limited.

Marx, K. (1954). *Capital, Vol 1*. London: Lawrence & Wishart.

Marx, K. (1963). *Theories of Surplus Value, Part I*. Moscow: Progress Publishers.

Meek, R. (1962). *The Economics of Physiocracy*. London: Allen & Unwin.

Meier, G. M. (1991). "The Political Economy of Policy Reform" in G. M. Meier (ed.): *Politics and Policy Making in Developing Countries*. San Francisco, CA: International Center for Economic Growth.

Mikesell, R. and J. Zinser (1973). "The Nature of the Savings Function in Developing Countries: A Survey of the Theoretical and Empirical Literature" *Journal of Economic Literature*, Vol. 11: 1-26.

Miller, M. (1981). "A Comparative Content Analysis of the Issue Content of the 1967 and the 1976 General Elections in Jamaica" in: Stone, C. and A. Brown (eds.): *Perspectives on Jamaica in the Seventies*. Kingston: Jamaica Publishing House.

Mitra, A. (1977). *Terms of Trade and Class Relations*. London: Frank Cass.

Moore, M. (1984). "Political Economy and the Rural-Urban Divide, 1767-1981" in J. Harriss and M. Moore (eds.): *Development and the Rural-Urban Divide*. London: Frank Cass.

Morrisson, C. and E. Thorbecke (1990) "The Concept of the Agricultural Surplus" *World Development*, Vol. 18: 1081-1095.

Myint, H. (1958). "The Classical Theory of Trade and the Underdeveloped Countries" *Economic Journal*, Vol. 68: 317-337.

Nabli, M. K. and J. B. Nugent (1989). *The New Institutional Economics and Development*. Amsterdam: North-Holland.

Nakajima, C. (1969). "Subsistence and Commerical Farms: Some Theoretical Models of Subjective Equilibrium" in C. R. Wharton (ed.): *Subsistence Agriculture and Economic Development*. Chicago: Aldine.

Nettleford, R. (1971). "Introduction" in R. Nettleford (ed.): *Norman Washington Manley and the New Jamaica. Selected Speeches and Writings, 1938-1968*. New York, NY: Africana Publishing Corporation.

NIP (1981). *National Income and Product, 1981*. Kingston: The Statistical Institute.

NIP (1984). *National Income and Product, 1984*. Kingston: The Statistical Institute.

North, D. C. (1990). *Institutions, Institutional Change and Economic Performance*. Cambridge: Cambridge University Press.

Nove, A. (1976). "The Political Economy of the Allende Regime" in P. O'Brien (ed.): *Allende's Chile*. New York, NY: Praeger.

O'Brien, D. P. (1975). *The Classical Economists*. Oxford: Clarendon Press.

Olson, M. (1965). *The Logic of Collective Action*. Cambridge, MA: Harvard University Press.

Owen, W. (1966). "The Double Developmental Squeeze on Agriculture" *American Economic Review*, Vol. 56: 43-70.

Palma, J. G. and M. Marcel (1989). "Kaldor on the 'Discreet Charm' of the Chilean Bourgeosie" *Cambridge Journal of Economics*, Vol. 13: 245-272.

Pasinetti, L. L. (1960). "A Mathematical Formulation of the Ricardian System" *Review of Economic Studies*, Vol. XXVII: 78-98.

Pasinetti, L. L. (1977). *Lectures on the Theory of Production*. London: Macmillan.

Pearson, H. W. (1957). "The Economy Has No Surplus" in K. Polanyi, C. M. Arensberg and H. W. Pearson (eds.): *Trade and Markets in the Early Empires*. New York, NY: The Free Press.

Persson, T. and G. Tabellini (1990). *Macroeconomic Policy, Credibility and Politics*. London: Harwood Academic Publishers.

Petty, W. (1963). *The Economic Writings of Sir William Petty, Vol. I*, ed by C. H. Hull. New York, NY: Kelley.

Phillips, J. D. (1966). "Estimating the Economic Surplus." Appendix to P. Baran and P. Sweezy: *Monopoly Capital*. New York, NY: Monthly Review. Reprinted as Chapter 3 in J. B. Davis (1992, ed.). *The Economic Surplus in Advanced Economies*. London: Edward Elgar.

Preobrazhensky, E. (1965). *The New Economics* (trans by Brian Pearce). Oxford: Clarendon Press.

Pyatt, G. and J. I. Round (1985, eds.): *Social Accounting Matrices. A Basis for Planning*. Washington DC: The World Bank.

Ranis, G. (1959). "The Financing of Japanese Economic Development" *The Economic History Review*, Vol. 11: 440-454.

Reid, S. (1977). "An Introductory Approach to the Concentration of Power in the Jamaican Corporate Economy and Notes on Its Origin" in C. Stone and A. Brown (eds.): *Essays on Power and Change in Jamaica*. Kingston: Jamaica Publishing House.

Reynolds, L. G. (1969). "Economic Development with Surplus Labour: Some Complications" *Oxford Economic Papers*, Vol. 21: 89-103.

Ricardo, D. (1951). *Principles of Political Economy and Taxation*. Edited by Piero Sraffa and Maurice Dobb. Cambridge: Cambridge University Press.

Riskin, C. (1975). "Surplus and Stagnation in Modern China" in Perkins, D. H. (ed.): *China's Modern Economy in Historical Perspective*. Stanford, CA: Stanford University Press.

RLF (1980). *Report on the Labour Force, 1981*. Kingston: The Statistical Institute.

RLF (1984). *Report on the Labour Force, 1984*. Kingston: The Statistical Institute.

Robbins, L. (1968). *The Theory of Economic Development*. London: Macmillan.

Roll, E. (1992). *A History of Economic Thought*. Fifth edition. London: Faber.

Roncaglia, A. (1978). *Sraffa and the Theory of Prices*. New York, NY: Wiley.

Rowley, C. K., R. D. Tollison and G. Tullock (1988). *The Political Economy of Rent-Seeking*. Boston, MA: Kluwer Academic Publishers.

Sah, R. K. and J. E. Stiglitz (1984). "The Economics of Price Scissors" *American Economic Review*, Vol. 74: 125-138.

Sah, R. K. and J. E. Stiglitz (1986). "The Economics of Price Scissors: Reply" *American Economic Review*, Vol. 76: 1195-1199.

Samuelson, P. A. (1982). "Quesnay's 'Tableau Économique' As a Theorist would Formulate it Today" in I. Bradley and M. Howard (eds): *Classical and Marxian Political Economy. Essays in Honour of Ronald L. Meek*. London: Macmillan.

Sawyer, M. C. (1982). *Macroeconomics in Question: The Keynesian-monetarist Orthodoxies and the Kaleckian Alternative*. Brighton: Wheatsheaf Books.

SBA (1973). *Länderkurzberichte: Jamaika, 1973*. Wiesbaden: Statistisches Bundesamt.

Schumpeter, J. A. (1954). *History of Economic Analysis*. London: Allen & Unwin.

Seers, D. (1976). "The Political Economy of National Accounting" in A. Cairncross and M. Puri (eds.): *Employment, Income Distribution and Development Strategy*. London: Macmillan.

Seers, D. (1983). *The Political Economy of Nationalism*. Oxford: Oxford University Press.

Sen, A. K. (1966). "Peasants and Dualism With or Without Surplus Labor" *Journal of Political Economy*, Vol. 74: 425-450.

Sharif, M. (1986). "The Concept and Measurement of Subsistence: A Survey of the Literature" *World Development*, Vol. 14: 555-577.

Smith, A. (1976). *An Inquiry into the Nature and Causes of the Wealth of Nations*. Edited by R H Campbell, A S Skinner and W B Todd. Oxford: Oxford University Press (the Glasgow edition).

Snyder, D. (1974). "Econometric Studies of Household Savings Behaviour in Developing Countries: A Survey" *Journal of Development Studies*, Vol. 10: 139-153.

Spiegel, H. W. (1983). *The Growth of Economic Thought*. Durham, NC: Duke University Press.

Sraffa, P. (1960). *Production of Commodities by Means of Commodities*. Cambridge: Cambridge University Press.

Stanfield, J. R. (1973). *The Economic Surplus and Neo-Marxism*. Lexington, MA: Heath & Co.

Stanfield, J. R. (1974). "A Revision of the Economic Surplus Concept" *Review of Radical Political Economics*, Vol. 6: 38-51.

Stanfield, J. R. (1992). "The Fund for Social Change" in J. B. Davis (ed.): *The Economic Surplus in Advanced Economies*. London: Edward Elgar.

Statistical Abstract (1984). Kingston: The National Planning Institute.

Stephens, E. H. and J. D. Stephens (1985). "Democratic Socialism and Bauxite in Jamaica" in P. Evans et al. (eds.): *States vs. Markets*. Beverly Hills, CA: Sage Publications.

Stephens, E. H. and J. D. Stephens (1986). *Democratic Socialism in Jamaica. The Political Movement and Social Transformation in Dependent Capitalism.* London: Macmillan.

Stone, C. (1980). *Democracy and Clientelism in Jamaica.* New Brunswick, NJ: Transaction Books.

Stone, C. (1981). "Party Voting Trends in Jamaica" in C. Stone and A. Brown (eds.): *Perspectives on Jamaica in the Seventies.* Kingston: Jamaica Publishing House.

Stone, C. (1982). *The Political Opinions of the Jamaican People.* Kingston: Jamaica Publishing House.

Stone, C. (1986). "Democracy and the State: The Case of Jamaica" in O. Davies (ed.): *The State in Caribbean Society.* Kingston: Department of Economics, University of the West Indies.

Stone, C. (1988). *Power and Policymaking in Jamaica.* Department of Political Sociology, University of the West Indies, Mona, mimeo.

Stone, R. (1985). "The Disaggregation of the Household Sector in the National Accounts" in G. Pyatt and J. I. Round (eds.): *Social Accounting Matrices. A Basis for Planning.* Washington DC: The World Bank.

Streeten, P. (1971). "Review of *Financing Development in Latin America,* edited by Keith Griffin" *Economic Journal,* Vol. 81: 1006-1009.

Todaro, M. P. (1969). "A Model of Labor Migration and Urban Unemployment in Less Developed Countries" *American Economic Review,* Vol. 59: 138-148.

de Vylder, S. (1974). *The Political Economy of the Rise and Fall of the Unidad Popular.* Stockholm: Unga filosofers förlag.

Walsh, V and H. Gram (1980): *Classical and Neoclassical Theories of General Equilibrium,* Oxford: Oxford University Press.

Yotopoulos, P. and J. Nugent (1976). *Economics of Development. Empirical Investigations.* New York, NY: Harper & Row.

Zarembka, P. (1970). "Marketable Surplus and Growth in the Dual Economy" *Journal of Economic Theory,* Vol. 2: 107-121.

Index

About the Author

ANDERS DANIELSON is Senior Lecturer in the Department of Economics, University of Lund, Sweden. Dr. Danielson has published *The Political Economy of Development Finance* (1993).